Pathway
TO
Freedom

A road map for individuals and organizations who
choose to be entrepreneurial in spirit and action.

Patrick and Adrienne Duffy

"What kind of dream shall awaken thee,
From your slumber sleep of security;
That you might rise within your own theatre,
Declaring your freedom,
And vowing to re-create your life;
As if for the first time."

Patrick Duffy

This book is dedicated to all our parents...
who have provided us with the opportunity to
experience the spirit of enterprise in action...
and to make a difference in the world.

And to all our children...
whose future dreams and missions in life are
irrevocably tied to us, planted as a seed within
our hearts.

To Laura, Alan & Matthew, January 18, 1996

May you enjoy tremendous success, happiness and prosperity along your Pathways to Freedom. Thank you for the gift of your friendship which we treasure in our hearts.

Love,
Adrienne & Patrick

Published by Big Futures Inc.
Printed in Edmonton, Canada

First printed 1995   5 4 3 2 1

Canadian Cataloguing in Publication Data
Duffy, Patrick, 1961 -
Pathway to freedom

Includes bibliographical references.
ISBN 1-896728-00-6

1. Success in business. 2. Entrepreneurship.
3. Self-actualization (Psychology)
 I. Duffy, Adrienne, 1956 -   II. Title.

HF5386.D83 1995   658.4'21   C95-911145-X

*If you would like further information about Big Futures Inc.
services and products, please phone (403) 487-7571
or fax (403) 489-7562.*

Acknowledgements

Our deepest appreciation to the many people whose support of this project helped our vision to become a reality.

To Mary Walters Riskin for her brilliant work in the editing of this book. Thank you for your invaluable expertise, insights, support and friendship throughout the project.

To Leland Val Van De Wall, in memoriam, for believing in us early on, and for leaving a legacy through your teachings.

To Dan Sullivan and Babs Smith, the founders of the Strategic Coach Inc., for your genius, mentorship, and inspiration. Thank you for your pioneering work.

To Susan Casault for bringing her creative design expertise to the cover, illustrations, and layout of the book. To Fred Katz for the cover photograph.

To Rollande Lauze-Duffy for her contribution to the editing process and for her ongoing love and support. To Bryan Pryde, Nora Cserny and Peggy Trainor for your assistance.

To our beautiful daughter Clara Ailene whose love, joy and laughter kept us going on many days.

It is impossible to name all the clients and business associates whose support over the years has contributed to help us find and cultivate our own "Pathway to Freedom." However, special thanks to: Frank Lovsin, Ken Haywood, and to Ian Alexander, Ed Brownfield, Charlie Grubisich, Marce Hall, John Jeffrey, Len Johnson, Bob Kinasewich, Jim McCool, John Mitchell, Ray Nelson, Blaine Nicholson, Ivan Radostits, Grant Smith, John Sweetnam, Ray Taillefer, the late Ted Tilden, and Gordon Wusyk.

Thank you to the countless numbers of people, known and unknown, whose commitment to finding their Pathways to Freedom inspired this book.

TABLE OF CONTENTS

TABLE OF CONTENTS

Part V: Building Extraordinary Relationships

Part VI: The Personal Organizing Structure

Part VII: Putting Your Freedom to Work for You

Epilogue

A Note to Readers

Many years ago we realized that if we wanted to make a difference through our work, we would have to get in touch with the questions of our times. We've been listening closely ever since, and one of the most challenging questions we have heard has been repeated over and over again by clients, friends and strangers, especially in recent years.

"If I am going to spend this much time and energy at work," they want to know, "how can I make sure that the time I spend is meaningful and significant?"

In our consultations with hundreds of individuals in numerous organizations and in a variety of circumstances, we have found that the answer to this question always lies within the person who asks it. The difficult part is developing a process to find the answer, and then to act on it.

The world is experiencing a phenomenon that can only be described as an entrepreneurial explosion. People from all walks of life and all backgrounds are discovering that by becoming more entrepreneurial — in spirit as well as in action — they can create a working life for themselves that allows them to express themselves as individuals while also providing them with economic stability.

The "Reader's Road Map" on the opposite page will give you an overview of the sections contained in the book. Sections One to Three give a wider context and explain how we have arrived today in what people choose to call a "no-job economy" — but what is actually an unprecedented opportunity for entrepreneurial activity. Sections Four through Seven focus on how you can put the Entrepreneurial Principle to work in your life. Whatever pathway through the book feels right for you is the one that you should take.

Over and over again, we have seen the spirit of enterprise allow individuals to move forward — in their work and all other areas of their life — with integrity, energy and purpose. This book is intended to guide and inspire you along your own personal pathway to freedom.

Enjoy!

Patrick and Adrienne Duffy

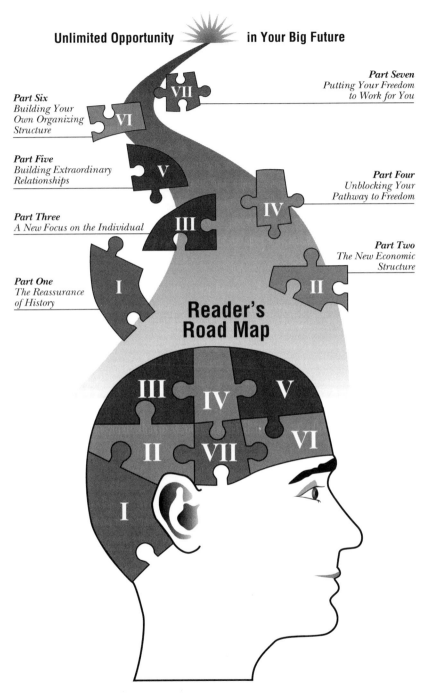

Unlimited Opportunity in Your Big Future

Part Seven
Putting Your Freedom
to Work for You

Part Six
Building Your
Own Organizing
Structure

Part Five
Building Extraordinary
Relationships

Part Four
Unblocking Your
Pathway to Freedom

Part Three
A New Focus on the Individual

Part Two
The New Economic
Structure

Part One
The Reassurance
of History

Reader's
Road Map

Becoming Entrepreneurial in
Spirit and Action

A Time of Great Choices

We are living at a crossroads in history, in a time of great choices. Historians, philosophers, artists, religious leaders, politicians, educators, and business people the world over agree that great changes are sweeping the globe. These changes are moving us toward a new world order, and causing nearly every institution on the earth to contemplate and evaluate its role, and to rethink its mandate.

This is not the first time that major institutions have been required by outside forces to transform themselves. Never before, however, have individuals been as enterprising, informed, and empowered as they are today — and never before have they played such a crucial role in determining how the institutions that surround them will affect their lives in the years that lie ahead.

Today we, as individuals, have an unprecedented opportunity to determine our own pathways to the future, both personally and professionally. We are indeed in a fortunate position.

This time of great choices is also a time of difficult questions. Today, particular problems and dilemmas present themselves to those of us who choose to take action in a changing world. Big questions touch on every aspect of our lives, from the social to the economic to the political. They are often complex and sophisticated, and they challenge our individual confidence, our perspectives, and our traditional attitudes.

Many of us are grappling in particular with the way we earn a living. The fundamental nature of "work" itself is going through a period of transformation, and its role in a knowledge-based economy has yet to be defined. These and other influences have led to many changes in the workplace — including the locations where work is conducted, the processes that are used to accomplish it, and the environments that provide its wider contexts.

In this time of change, it is necessary for each of us to develop perspectives on our working lives, and on our personal lives as well, that are both wide-ranging and enduring. A set of new attitudes, new mindsets, new ways of looking at activities, and new organizing structures are needed by individuals who wish to be effective in the future.

> **"When you discover your essential nature and know who you really are, *in that knowing itself* is the ability to fulfill any dream you have [...]."**
>
> — *Deepak Chopra*
> *The Seven Spiritual Laws of Success*

Finding a pathway through the difficult questions and great choices offered to us by this period in history is not a journey for the faint of heart. In order to be effective and to adapt to the new world order, we must make contact with our own individual spirit of enterprise. It is this spirit which will provide us with the ability to explore new views, to discover new methods, and to find new pathways. It will allow us to develop confidence, based on the belief that there is a place for us in the new world — now, and in the future.

The Pioneering Spirit

Some of us are actual descendants of the explorers and settlers who came to this continent in the 17th, 18th, and 19th centuries, and most of our families emigrated from other parts of the world to settle in North America at some point in the past. It is not difficult for most North Americans to relate to the pioneering spirit of our predecessors.

The spirit of the pioneers who settled North America embodied a fortuitous blend of attitudes, values and skills. Their approach can be helpful to us today as we face unknown changes in our work and in our personal lives, and can also serve as a metaphor for the journey on which new entrepreneurs are about to embark.

If you had been out walking in Independence, Missouri on a sunlit morning in the summer of 1865, you would have seen a parade of wagons pass you, filled with people, supplies, and dreams. Hundreds of pioneers were setting off on a long expedition to a new life.

No doubt you would have seen concern and even fear on the faces of some of these travelers. The expressions of others would have been defiant, despite the odds they

Independence Rock, Casper, Wyoming

UNKNOWN

KNOWN

Pioneers declaring themselves along the Oregon Trail

knew they faced. Some would have looked surprisingly confident and optimistic. It is certain that most of them looked back toward the east — the known world — from time to time, wondering if their place in life truly lay ahead.

No matter what expressions they wore, these pioneers displayed the height of human enterprise and faith. Each day they traveled to a new land. Each day they needed to find new sources of water and food. Each night they cooked their meals in a new place, often not certain how safe their lives, their families, and their possessions might be. With each new sunrise, they saw a new horizon. Each day they faced a new world.

These people could not have prepared themselves fully for their journeys. Many methods of survival had to be learned on the road. They were willing and able to "learn as they went" because, in spite of the unexpected turns, the misfortunes and challenges of an unknown pathway, their vision for a new life endured.

The pioneers exemplified the triumph of long-term perspective over short-term circumstance, which allowed their pioneering spirit victory over their fears of a great unknown.

Along the Oregon Trail, many of these pioneers carved their names into a natural marker now known as Independence Rock. It has become a memorial to the spirit of these people, and it can be seen to represent an affirmation on their parts: they declared that a future in the new world order offered them greater opportunity than did the known world from which they had come.

Whether they traveled forward out of religious, family, economic, social, political or enterprising reasons, by their actions they declared themselves — and declared their relationship with the future.

> **"A man on the frontier must make his own decisions and act upon them. Consequently, there was no subservience. Those who solve problems for themselves become confident. They trust in their own abilities."**
>
> *— Louis L'Amour,*
> *speaking on the Oregon Trail, in Frontier*

The legacy of the declarations of these pioneers, and of the choices they made, can be seen everywhere around us: our lifestyles were made possible by their dreams. The rich inheritance they — and the millions of immigrants who followed them — left to us is more than just physical, however. Their legacy embodies the spirit of enterprise itself. In this time of great choices and great questions, we will need to put this spirit to work again — for us and for future generations.

Declare Yourself

As we move into a challenging economic landscape and new world order, our Independence Rock does not lie in the realm of geography as much as it does in the spirit of enterprise. Today, individuals are carving their names in all of the corporate registries in the states and provinces of North America by establishing small businesses and private enterprises. They are choosing pathways of personal responsibility, believing that the potential for greater creativity, significance and freedom lies ahead, in new systems and new structures, rather than in the political and corporate hierarchies of the past.

Each of us must decide how we will declare ourselves today. We must decide whether we are to establish contact with the spirit of enterprise which is certainly within us. We must decide whether we are ready to put our faith in our own abilities. We must decide whether we can trust our own commitment enough to overcome our fears. We must decide whether we are prepared to discover, explore, and then settle successfully into the new world order.

The Entrepreneurial Mind

When the world is stable and orderly, teaching people what they need to *know* and what they need to *do* often serves as adequate guidance. With this information, they can develop the necessary confidence and competence to become successful in their work and in their lives. During the past century, our society has been particularly successful at teaching these two approaches.

Today, however, we are moving into an economy that is based on knowledge and information, and our world lacks stability and order. Where there is a lack of pre-dictability and control, a third skill becomes crucial. People must also learn how to *be*.

Learning "how to be" means developing a system of beliefs, attitudes, mindsets and habits that will make our future actions and practices as fulfilling, effective and successful as possible. In this endeavor, we have a useful role model in the traditional entrepreneur.

Successful entrepreneurs have always, of course, created business structures and working environments that have allowed them to prosper economically. However, it is not their physical organization, but their beliefs and attitudes to which we need to pay particular attention at the moment.

Entrepreneurs have historically begun their learning process by developing *themselves*, rather than by focusing exclusively on knowledge and action. Their values, attitudes and beliefs have caused them to question accepted business and educational perspectives, to forge ahead to fulfill their own dreams, and to anticipate the future so that they will play a significant role in it, and enjoy a freer life.

Entrepreneurs take personal responsibility for developing their own integrated learning structures — and they finance this personal education with their time, effort, and enterprise.

As we begin to make the new spirit of learning part of our own way of thinking, our levels of confidence and enthusiasm will immediately increase. An entrepreneurial approach improves not only our attitudes toward our work, but also toward our lives. It allows us to begin to shape our futures to meet our wants and needs, to make significant contributions to others, and to live richer, freer lives.

A New Spirit of Learning:

Learning with integrity by fully integrating values, attitudes and mindsets so that the learning process builds confidence.

Knowledge
Learning what "To Know"

Skills
Learning how "To Do"

Attitudes Mindsets and Values
Learning how "To Be"

Entrepreneurial Spirit Expressed in "Be" Attitudes	Entrepreneurial Spirit Expressed in Mindsets
• Be Personally Responsible • Be Committed • Be Passionate • Be Unique • Be Significant • Be Free	• Visionary • Creative • Strategic • Relationship-oriented

Foundation of Core Values

Evaluating the Health of Your Entrepreneurial Spirit

We all have a relationship with the Entrepreneurial "Be" Attitudes and Mindsets because they are intrinsic to our human spirit. However, it can be valuable to determine the quality of that relationship in order to identify improvement opportunities. Please complete the following exercise to evaluate your status.

ENTREPRENEURIAL "BE" ATTITUDES

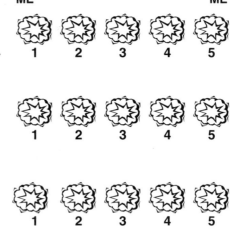

	Not at all like ME				A lot like ME

1. I am personally responsible for the results in my life and for shaping my future.

   1   2   3   4   5

2. I bring the spirit of commitment to all key relationships and activities in my life.

   1   2   3   4   5

3. I am passionate about discovering and actualizing my life mission.

   1   2   3   4   5

4. I believe that I have been endowed with unique talents and abilities.

   1   2   3   4   5

	Not at all like ME				A lot like ME

5. I desire to make a difference in the world.

    1   2   3   4   5

6. I thirst for greater freedom in my life.

    1   2   3   4   5

ENTREPRENEURIAL MINDSETS

Not at all like ME   A lot like ME

1. I have a strong vision of what I want to accomplish in every significant area of my life over the next three years.

    1   2   3   4   5

2. I create opportunities to express my creativity in my work.

    1   2   3   4   5

3. I set goals to focus my energy and measure my progress in all key areas of my life.

    1   2   3   4   5

4. I believe my personal and professional success depends on the extraordinary relationships I cultivate in my life.

    1   2   3   4   5

THE REASSURANCE OF HISTORY

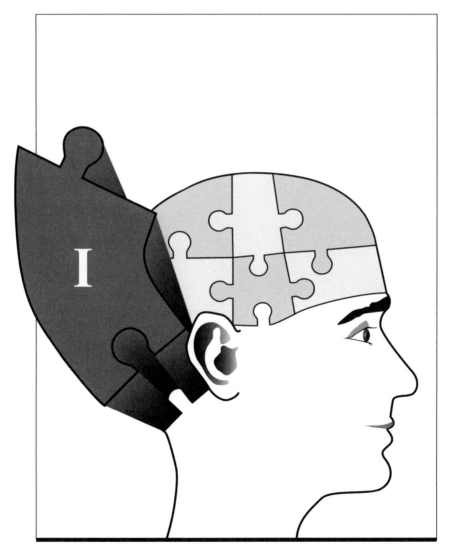

The Reassurance of History

When you consider the tremendous transitions our world has undergone during the last 4500 years, we are fortunate not only to be alive, but to have been given the opportunity to prosper. For the fourth time in human history, a significant advance in the way humans communicate is precipitating global transformation.

Dan Sullivan identifies these transition periods, where breakthroughs in communication lead to major social change, as "Great Crossover" periods. Each of the three Great Crossovers that preceded the one we are experiencing today dramatically affected the way humans related to one another, and in particular the way they organized themselves. The Fourth Great Crossover is no exception.

The First Great Crossover followed the development of spoken language, which historians date at approximately 50,000 B.C.

The Second Great Crossover began when language evolved from mere pictographs, and was first written down, likely in Sumer circa 2500 B.C.

The Third Great Crossover was precipitated by the invention of the printing press, when mass production of printed language became possible. This is generally timed with the release of the Gutenberg Bible in 1456 A.D.

The Fourth Great Crossover in communication began with the invention of the microchip in 1958, establishing digital language as the new format of information storage and exchange.

An examination of the first three Crossovers shows the powerful relationship that exists between human communication and human organizing structures. This truth has dramatic implications for us today. Although the future can never be totally predicted, by studying changes that occurred during previous Crossovers and extrapolating from current trends, we can draw fairly solid conclusions as to how societal organizing structures will be altered during this period.

The Fourth Great Crossover will transform every business and every political system in the world, but it will have its greatest impact on the individual. It will alter not only how we choose to earn a living, but ultimately how we choose to live our lives.

To appreciate the magnitude of this period of change, we need to be aware of the effects of previous Crossovers on the way societies functioned. By looking at past systems of human organization, and the dramatic impact on them of changes in communication, we can begin to

understand the unprecedented character of the era in which we find ourselves today.

Change is natural and essential. Without it, evolution cannot occur. Since the beginning of civilization, humans have survived and even thrived in the midst of change. An examination of the past assures us that we are capable of dealing with the kinds of change we are experiencing today, no matter how far reaching the consequences.

History is on our side.

CHAPTER ONE

The Societal Organizing Structure

Organizing structures may be individual or societal. Historically, societal organizing structures have predominated, and individuals have been expected to align their beliefs and their behaviors with those of society as a whole.

An "organizing structure" is a model of human organization which is based on a specific set of:

- beliefs

- rules, and

- guidelines for behavior.

Historically speaking, the Fourth Crossover presents humans with the greatest opportunity ever to develop their own individual, or personal, organizing structures. A brief look at the history of human organization places the changes that are taking place today into dramatic perspective.

Societal Organizing Structures

Societal organizing structures are designed, dictated and enforced by particular authoritative bodies.

These bodies gain the power to organize human communities in part from their relationship with knowledge — they alone have access to knowledge, in some cases they control its distribution, and they have the confidence to interpret it on behalf of society as a whole.

While there have always been many advantages to societal organizing structures, they do allow the few to control the many. In order for hierarchical systems like these to function effectively, it is necessary for those "at the top" to invent and enforce rules and regulations, and for those "below" to live by them. The leaders of authoritative bodies are accorded the position of custodians of social direction, conformity and order.

The activities of individuals within organized societies — from their educations to their lifestyles — are expected to conform to the objectives of the structure, and to adhere to the rules contained within it.

Religious groups and governments are examples of major authoritative bodies that have established and successfully maintained societal organizing structures for long periods in the past.

Societal Organization by Religion

Seven hundred years ago, as the Third Great Crossover (the printed word) approached, much of the world was organized by religion. While monarchs and other political potentates had their sway, most were highly influenced by their religious leaders. Throughout the world, a host of religious bodies directed the lives of millions of individual believers. Their power was as much economic and social as it was spiritual.

The influence of Roman Catholicism on Western civilization provides us with one example. Followers of the Roman Catholic Church were expected to conform to

the Church's organizing structure, which included a system of beliefs as well as rules and guidelines for behavior. The Church had been able to gain its power, and was able to maintain it, because it controlled the language of, the access to, and the interpretation of, knowledge.

Within the societal organizing structure of the Church, which was enforced by the clergy, the individual had little flexibility or freedom. Those who stepped outside established guidelines attracted a good deal of undesirable attention. Expressing thoughts that were inconsistent with Church interpretation was considered blasphemous, and in some instances it carried the penalty of death.

The domination of the Roman Catholic Church was eroded by the invention of the printing press in the mid-1400s. Individuals who could read could now interpret the written word for themselves, which led to the development of new philosophies and systems of belief. The decline of the power of the Church as the primary director of societal organization was underway.

Societal Organization by Politics

As the power of religious bodies declined with the dissemination of knowledge, the primary societal organizing structure of western society gradually evolved from a religious base to a political one. Over the next 250 to 350 years, the Nation States emerged, and the western world moved toward democratic rule — government of the people, by the people.

The beliefs and behaviors of society were now controlled not by religious edict, but by documents drawn up by legislative bodies that quickly grew in both size and number. Constitutional decrees and lists of regulations began to govern every aspect of human life — from the rights of individuals to taxation. Individual and family attitudes towards life and work began to focus increasingly on order and control, and the saying, "A well-ordered life is a successful life," became a catchphrase in churches, businesses and schools.

As legislative bodies introduced increasing numbers of social programs and social systems, many individuals came to believe that they were incapable of managing their own lives without substantial input from the political organizing structure and its related sub-structures.

While this system tended to move society forward as a whole, as the religious system had previously done, individual initiative and potential were once again de-emphasized, and even repressed, by externally imposed beliefs, values and convictions.

This externally imposed order led the individual to see the shaping of his or her own future as someone else's responsibility. Many people began to believe that as long as they completed certain tasks, and were consistently productive and loyal, their futures would be looked after by those in authority.

The political operating principle that evolved throughout the late 19th and early 20th centuries has been described by Peter Drucker, in his book, *Post-Capitalist Society*, as "individual salvation by society." As voters demanded and received increasing numbers of entitlements, political organizing structures were accorded increasing responsibility for the guidance, direction and control of the lives of their citizens.

Societal Organization Today

For four centuries, the dominant organizing structure of the western world has been political in nature. Most private organizations imitate the hierarchical structure of public institutions and, until the current generation, most of us accepted this structure quite willingly. The long-term rewards made doing so worthwhile.

Our schools — most of which operate on the same bureaucratic, top-down basis as most other institutions — have been the training ground for our conformity to "the system." If we learned the rules, we were taught, if we were loyal and worked hard, our rewards would include secure jobs, generous standards of living, a host of benefit programs and comfortable retirements.

Today — as far too many of us have learned from personal experience — the political structure no longer works. Gone are the security, the certainty, and the safety nets that protected generations of workers before us. The most loyal and hard-working employee — and the one with the greatest seniority — is still vulnerable to the pink slip.

Today, bureaucratically structured school systems no longer prepare us for the future. Governments can no longer afford to subsidize our medical bills, protect us from economic change, or provide us with pension benefits from retirement until the day we die. Even religious organizations — themselves often structured hierarchically — are having difficulty renewing themselves, much less providing spiritual guidance to the people.

The reign of the politically based organizing structure is coming to an end. As was true with the demise of the religion-based structure before it, the effect of this development will be felt by the individual in all areas of life. For many of us today, however, one of the primary signs of the impact of the Fourth Crossover is the effect it is having in the workplace.

CHAPTER TWO

The Evolution of the "Job"

>⋅⊢⊹⋅⊙⋅⟨⊹⊢⋅≺

When we look at the history of socioeconomic models that have predominated in the western world, we see that the "job" is a relatively recent phenomenon. The word was not even used to mean "a position of employment" until the 19th century, and the concept as we know it today is largely a legacy of the Industrial Age.

It is obvious that today's corporate and institutional upheavals require us to re-examine, on a very basic level, the whole notion of how income is earned by individuals. Those of us who will move ahead in the new economy will benefit from replacing traditional ways of thinking about work and income with an individual entrepreneurial approach. A review of the evolution of western society's pervasive "job-filler" mentality will assist us in this endeavor.

The Crafts and Trades

Entrepreneurism is not new. However, its practice has been more common during certain periods of history than others. Whether the business was suited to the talents and nature of the entrepreneur was often immaterial.

Some of the earliest entrepreneurs were the tradesmen and craftsmen of society. While the crafts and trades that were prevalent between two and four hundred years ago were strictly regulated by associations and guilds, the system allowed qualified masters to attract income based on their individual talents and skills.

Trade apprenticeships were one of the first organized systems through which individuals could access information that was economically valuable. In order to learn how to apply knowledge to create a livelihood, apprentices studied under masters for as long as six to eight years.

At least two customs discouraged wide dissemination of the information that apprentices obtained. First, trade practices could only be demonstrated by a master within the confines of the workplace, and those who became privy to these techniques were expected to keep them secret. Second, as apprenticeships were passed from generation to generation in order to protect the economic standing of the family, their availability was largely limited to immediate family members.

"In nearly all the towns the exercise of the different arts and trades was concentrated within the hands of a small number of masters (maîtrise) [...] who alone had the privilege, to the exclusion of all other citizens, of making or selling the objects of the special trade of which they had exclusive privilege."

— *Leon Say, a member of the French Academy,*
in <u>*Turgot*</u>*, 1888*

The invention of the printing press permitted invasions on the secrecy of the crafts and trades. Between 1751 and 1772, Denis Diderot and Jean D'Alembert attempted to capture all knowledge in their *Encyclopédie*, and one of their initiatives was to catalogue the details of the practices of crafts and trades.

L'Encyclopédie was an early example of economically valuable information appearing in printed format — and as such, it contributed to the societal transformation that marked the impact of the Third Great Crossover.

Suddenly anyone who could read — or who knew someone who could — could learn the techniques of specific trades and crafts. Power had moved from the masters to the people, and now individuals had a far greater selection of entrepreneurial occupations from which to choose than they had ever had before.

Time and Effort

As individual land rights and civic rights evolved through the 15th to 19th centuries, and as the Nation States developed democratic rule, entrepreneurial opportunities expanded beyond trades, hospitality, agriculture, and other services. Entrepreneurism, primarily in the form of agrarian enterprise, reached its peak in the late 1800s.

During the Industrial Revolution, with the growth of manufacturing and the need to find workers to increase the output of large factories, the "job" as we know it today was born.

Factory workers were expected to put in certain numbers of hours every work day, completing a clear set of tasks, ordered in a certain way, in order to create a consistent and productive result. Their incomes were tied to both their ability to consistently and effectively complete a series of tasks (effort), while being efficient in terms of the productive results created during the day (time). The time-and-effort view of the workplace quickly became entrenched because it created order and focus within a productive environment.

The Industrial Era took the time-and-effort model to new heights. As information with economic value became increasingly available, the hunger shifted from accessibility to application. Increased output was the goal of factory managers and, thanks in part to the widespread influence of the Protestant work ethic, productivity became the measure by which the success of workers was assessed.

Western society quickly adapted to an employer-employee model that was characterized by regular work and steady incomes. The system was reinforced by two world wars, which required large segments of society to organize themselves for the purpose of survival. Within a few decades, most people had grown so used to the concept of going out and working every day that they had begun to feel they were entitled to do so.

The most profound legacy of this period has been the creation of the middle class, where a heavy emphasis is placed on education, job security, and the importance of institutions both political and public. The middle class has established a vast array of rules for itself, including guidelines for success in individual and family life.

The influence of the middle class, and the "entitlement" thinking that coloured the attitudes of much of western society, led to the greatest period of power and profit that has ever been enjoyed by western political organizing structures.

CHAPTER THREE

Social Programs and Entitlement

The technological advancement that marked the Industrial Age was directed at greater productivity and further innovation, but it had major shortcomings. It diminished the dignity and efficacy of the individual person.

In factories and on farms, human productivity was increasingly compared with the output of machines. With productivity the measure of one's economic value, the future role for humans in the marketplace became increasingly exacting.

Controversy and consternation over this issue grew as the economic impact of the Industrial Revolution began to influence the structure of society. Near the end of the 19th century, writers across Europe were noting the failure of the Revolution to create meaningful, fulfilling roles for individuals outside of their potential to contribute time and effort. The growth of Marxism and similar movements can be attributed to concerns of this nature that were widespread at the time.

In 1880, Prince Otto von Bismarck of Germany attempted to create a new image for the industrial worker. In response to political pressure from those who advocated change for the good of the "common man," and in order to dignify the value of workers and protect them physically, he inaugurated state-sponsored welfare initiatives. These included health insurance, a form of worker's compensation, and old-age pensions.

In the early 1900s, the British followed suit with the introduction of unemployment insurance, and in the midst of the Depression of the 1930s, Franklin Delano Roosevelt introduced Social Security to the United States as part of the New Deal.

Although economic protection for the individual by government may initially have been necessary and well intentioned, it began a cycle of political controls of the free market that led to widespread belief in individual entitlement.

Employment came to be seen as a natural condition to which each citizen had a right. In addition, the thinking went, if the Nation State controlled the free-market economy, and the free-market economy created unemployment, then the Nation State must be responsible for the unemployed. This attitude was reinforced by the introduction of unemployment insurance. People began to believe that unemployment must be a temporary and undesirable condition, or governments would not insure against it.

In the atmosphere of fear that arose from the poverty of the Depression years, workers felt betrayed. They believed they "deserved" economic guarantees, including job security and social safety nets. That is what they wanted for the future.

In response, between 1930 and 1970, governments introduced a range of additional social-welfare programs and economic initiatives that reinforced a view of political responsibility. These included universal health care, full workers' compensation and expanded unemployment insurance. Governments created jobs through developing mega-projects, and they became deeply involved in the regulation of markets.

As the role of the Nation State grew larger in the life of each individual, the concept Drucker has described as "salvation by society" took firm hold. The average person came to believe that the government was responsible for the economy, and for managing many other areas of life as well.

In order to fully appreciate the magnitude of the changes required in our thinking processes today, we must become fully aware of the consequences of the entitlement attitudes that have developed in the past sixty years.

"I should like to state to you the effect that this projection of government in business would have upon our system of self-government and our economic system. That effect would reach to the daily life of every man and woman. It would impair the very basis of liberty and freedom not only for those left outside the expanded bureaucracy but for those embraced within it.... Bureaucracy is ever desirous of spreading its influence and its power. You cannot extend the mastery of Government over the daily working life of a people without at the same time making it the master of the peoples' souls and thoughts."

— *Herbert C. Hoover, 1928*

The Promise

Primarily as a result of government direction, most of us have grown up with the conviction that "jobs" lead to "security." This is The Promise. Despite the fact that it is rarely verbalized, The Promise has become intrinsic to our system of beliefs and deeply embedded in our collective psyche. We have been raised to believe that if we fit ourselves into the work place and then work hard throughout our lives — adapting our wants, needs and values to the system — we will receive financial security in return.

Our educational institutions have, for the most part, been based on the principle that those who are "trained" or "educated" will find positions in the work force — and that those positions will provide them with security for the remainder of their lives.

While The Promise delivered for many, many years, it is becoming increasingly clear today that the system in which we have been raised to believe is no longer functional. As traditional occupations continue to decline in number, society as a whole is finding it necessary to move away from the job-security mentality. In fact, "job security" in its traditional sense is becoming an anachronism.

This development is not entirely negative from a historical point of view. During the thousands of years of human socioeconomic evolution, job security has hardly been a consistent destination or goal — nor has it been a pre-requisite for that evolution to take place. If recent events in Eastern Europe, Latin America and other parts of the world are any indicator, we, as human beings, seem to want greater individual freedom and personal responsibility.

"Freedom" is usually not part of the traditional job description. If we intend to make meaningful progress, we must be willing to consider other attitudes and mind-sets about work and our relationship with it.

Beyond Job Security

The world is changing around us, and if we wish to become truly successful in the new economy, we must change as well. The Promise has left us with a legacy of thought processes relating to security that most of us have carried with us from childhood. Now we must learn to present ourselves as unique and separate individuals, and to accept economic responsibility for our own futures. In order to do this effectively, we must modify many of our attitudes and our traditional thinking patterns.

Despite the sense of betrayal we may feel at the loss of a long-held belief, we need to remind ourselves that there are positive aspects to relinquishing our hold on The Promise — and its hold on us. Current conditions present us with an opportunity for liberation. Today more often our options allow us to interact with the world as individuals rather than as cogs in an economic machine.

The opportunity to develop as individuals may have been forced on us by time and circumstance, but it is one that many of us find appealing.

THE NEW ECONOMIC ORGANIZATION

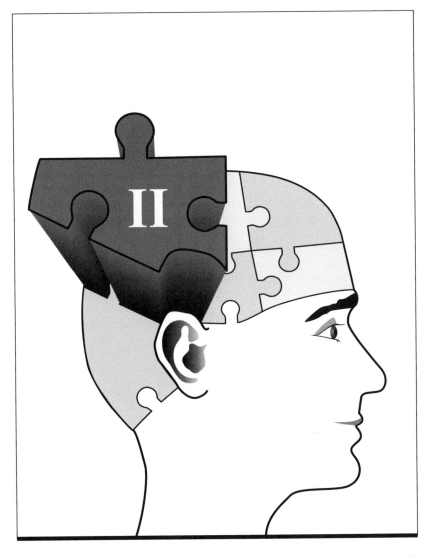

The New Economic Organization

Between 1900 and 1960, as governments were accorded increasing responsibility and power by the people, national economies became closely associated with national identities. Governments throughout the world — and their electorates — operated as though free markets were geographically based, and therefore fell naturally within the realm of regional and national political regulation and control. It became second nature to refer to the economy of one nation as totally distinct from that of another.

> **"Nowadays you have one worldwide stock exchange. Nobody is controlling it. You have one worldwide money market. Nobody is controlling it. The Central Banks are still living in the world of the 1970s, some in the 1960s."**
>
> *— Economist and former German Chancellor*
> *Helmut Schmidt,*
> *on the diminishing role of government*
> *in international financial markets*

For many years, governments did appear to control economies, and did seem to provide economic security to their citizens. Particularly during elections, political parties reinforced the perception of the Nation State as all-powerful, and responsible for the economic well

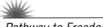

being of individuals and their families. Success at the polls was typically related to election promises that presumed the ability of governments to control and direct the economy.

A new age of global economic trade began in 1971 when the American dollar was allowed to "float" free of the gold standard, and it was hastened by technological advances. The microchip has allowed the instantaneous spread of information around the world, and economic exchange can no longer be contained by political borders. Today, super computers in New York alone electronically manage approximately $2 trillion a day. Compare this with the Gross Domestic Product of Canada, which was approximately $566 billion for the entire year of 1993.

In *The Death of Money*, Joel Kurtzman points out that "it is now far easier and faster to move $1 billion from New York to Tokyo than to move a truckload of lettuce and grapes across the California-Arizona line." If an exclusive relationship between governments and national economies ever existed, it no longer does today. The power of the free-market system is now far greater than that of any political organizing structure.

Simultaneously, governments have become incapable of shouldering the responsibility we have accorded them for the livelihoods of individual citizens. Social-welfare programs are being cut to the bone. Thousands and thousands of lost jobs — including many within governments themselves — are putting terminal strains on unemployment insurance and other safety nets. The pace and magnitude of change in the workplace is so overwhelming that traditional government strategies like make-work projects are about as effective as umbrellas in an avalanche.

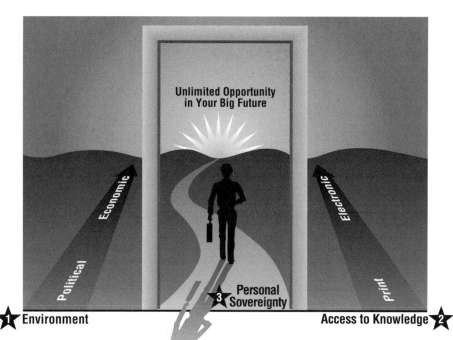

Unlimited Opportunity in Your Big Future

Economic

Political

Electronic

Print

3 Personal Sovereignty

⭐ **1** Environment

Access to Knowledge **2** ⭐

The Great Personal Crossover

1. **Environment** - We are now moving from the political organizing structure that has dominated our society, to an economic organizing structure.

2. **Access to Knowledge** - Thanks to electronic and digital advances, the printed word is no longer the only way to store, access and transfer information.

3. **Personal Sovereignty** - The sovereign individual will be responsible for creating personal security and providing leadership and direction in all significant areas of his or her life.

The Shift to an Economy Base

We have already seen a number of effects of the shift from a political organizing structure to a structure that is economically oriented, and is based on the free market system. It has made us less able to predict and control our circumstances, and it has resulted in confusion and distress. The shift has affected far more than our economic outlook. It has challenged the traditional roles of institutions, families, and individuals.

Some key developments in the economic and communications fields which have undermined stability and confounded traditional expectations are:

- the capability for instantaneous media coverage of global events 24 hours every day;

- the immediate impact of news coverage on financial markets; and

- the introduction of the personal computer, which has allowed individual access to financial information from around the world that was previously available only to institutions, governments, and large corporations.

An economic organizing structure is constantly and exclusively focused on finding the highest possible value and the greatest possible return for resources. It has little concern for borders, voters or social programs. Today, investors have as much or more influence as governments on the interest-rate levels which have replaced the gold standard as a primary influence in economic exchange. Political leaders have come to recognize that the views of the investment community worldwide must be considered when any important domestic economic policy is being developed.

This has dramatic implications for the individual. Since an economic organizing structure is concerned exclusively with "real value," and the definition of "real value" changes daily in every industry, no longer can any one person, corporation or government afford to feel complacent in any field of economic endeavor. Throughout the world, the economic security of every individual will ultimately come to rest with that individual, which means that people everywhere must become increasingly responsible and accountable to and for themselves. Their performances will be measured by their ongoing ability to generate value in their chosen areas of economic focus. The microchip has generated a variety of tools that can help them to accomplish this consistently.

An Economy Based on Knowledge

The invention of the microchip has made possible, for the first time in human history, the accurate, inexpensive and effective transmission of information and money around the world. For this reason, the microchip is at the centre of the current global transition from a political organizing structure to an economic organizing structure.

Thanks to the microchip, the world has become one giant, interconnected marketplace of money, people, commodities, products, knowledge and services. When the opportunity exists to create greater value for any resource by moving it across the world, individuals and institutions are able to do so instantaneously, and with all relevant information at their fingertips.

Over the last 30 years, the microchip's capacity has increased according to a pattern that was forecast many years ago by Gordon Moore. In 1965, Moore predicted that the processing power of microchips would double every eighteen months.

In October, 1995, the *The Financial Post Magazine* reported that the microchip "used in the first generation of IBM PCs packed 29,000 transistors onto a single chip. The 286 which followed quadrupled that to 134,000. The 386 doubled it again to 275,000. The introduction of the 486, followed in turn by the Pentium, ushered in a new inflationary era in the transistor-count department — a whopping 3.1 million."

In 1990, for the first year, capital spending on the information economy (computers and telecommunications equipment) surpassed capital spending on all other parts of the industrial infrastructure in the United States of America. As a result of this landmark occurrence, economists are proclaiming that the U.S. economy is being transformed from an industrial base to an information base.

These figures dramatically illustrate the high priority we humans, as a group, have assigned to developing the free-market system through cheaper and more effective ways of handling and interpreting information. We also continue to see the impact of the microchip on our individual lives, as we quickly move beyond the personal computer to the Personal Digital Assistant (PDA). The PDA, a major expansion of lap-top computer capability, will soon become the primary tool by which people manage themselves and their work.

Thanks to developments of this nature, an environment is being created in which individuals who combine creativity with a strategic process have the greatest opportunity to generate economic value.

The Importance of Personal Confidence

It will take time for society to reorganize itself and its attitudes so that technology as a tool of productivity may be fully utilized. It is already becoming apparent, however, that productivity today is tied to personal confidence and the ability to manage relationships, as much as to computer competence.

The new economic organizing structure is notable because for the first time in history there will be no single regulatory or guiding body — no church or government — that will set the rules and dictate how individuals will or should respond to change.

The absence of leadership structures has tremendous implications for all of society, but it is on individual and family life that the greatest impact will be felt. As existing institutional sources of support and guidance continue their decline, personal confidence will increasingly become the most vital personal and economic resource available to us as individuals.

In *The Post-Capitalist Society,* Peter Drucker stresses the urgency for individuals to develop new attitudes in their approach to work. He says, "The end of the belief in salvation by society surely marks an inward turning. It makes possible renewed emphasis on the individual, the person. It may even lead, at least we can so hope, to a return to individual responsibility."

Only through accepting greater personal responsibility will individuals generate the confidence they need to discover their pathways to the future. The new economic organizing structure has brought with it the need for a new definition of the role of the individual, and of his or her relationship with work.

The fact that governments and other institutions can no longer meet our expectations does not mean that we must surrender these expectations. What it does mean is that we must learn to look to new sources for our economic direction, and for our personal security.

The new economic structure, and the demands it makes of us for personal accountability, combine to make this one of the richest moments in history for the development of individual enterprise and an entrepreneurial approach.

CHAPTER ONE

The Impact of the Fourth Crossover

Abrupt transformations to systems of human information management led to three Great Crossovers in the past, and the invention of the microchip has now precipitated the Fourth.

While, relatively speaking, the effects of the first three crossovers on human civilization were as dramatic as those of the Fourth will be, there are three major differences between this Crossover and the ones that preceded it.

1. The major effects of this period of transition will be seen over the span of a single lifetime.

Individuals who are alive today will witness the most dramatic effects of the Fourth Crossover. In our lifetimes we have already seen unprecedented change on both individual and global levels, and the acceleration and intensity of this change will continue for at least another quarter of a century.

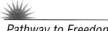
In order to prevent being buffeted or even swept away by the changes that surround us, each of us will need to transform a tremendous number of beliefs, attitudes, habits and practices that affect both the personal and professional components of our lives. With a solid base of self-knowledge and self-confidence, we will become capable of working within the context of global change to enhance our individual lives.

2. The Fourth Crossover will have an unprecedented impact on individual lives.

The first three Crossovers had their primary effects on groups and institutions. Individual citizens felt the impact of these Crossovers through the political and religious bodies that took the lead in restructuring society.

With no dominant authoritative body to depend on any longer, we will feel the effects of the Fourth Great Crossover far more personally than our predecessors felt the effects of previous ones. We will become aware of the impact of this Crossover in every area of our lives.

By gaining confidence from a self-designed and self-directed life — in other words, by developing a truly entrepreneurial approach — we will learn how to contribute vision, creativity and the ability to be strategic toward the resolution of many problems — whether they are ours alone, or those of society as a whole.

3. In the new world order, individuals will need to accept responsibility for their own lives.

The need for individual accountability and responsibility is the most significant difference between the Fourth Great Crossover and those that have preceded it. It is as

responsible individuals that we will play a key role in society's reformation.

In order to determine our economic roles and create organizing structures for our own lives, each of us will need to develop self-direction, rather than relying on guidance from organizations or even other individuals. While accepting responsibility for our lives requires focus and willpower, ultimately it liberates us, allowing us to develop our full potential.

CHAPTER TWO

The Conditions of Change

Three major trends can be identified as society shifts from a political to an economic organizing structure.

1. The Central Catalyst for change during this Crossover period is economics.

Due to rapid advances in technology, economic change is being experienced with increasing speed and intensity. The value of all goods and services will ultimately be determined exclusively by the free-market system, which will operate much more independently of political influence than it does today. As we are already becoming aware, economics will ultimately drive politics, rather than the other way around. This will affect not only the economic area of our lives, but all other areas as well.

2. Individuals will need to become responsible for aspects of their lives that were previously protected by politically generated programs.

As the political structure becomes less capable of protecting citizens economically, and less effective in organizing and directing them, individuals will be required to take on greater personal responsibility for themselves and their families.

Those who continue to depend on outside forces for their security will experience effects that are increasingly chaotic and difficult to control. Entrepreneurs, on the other hand, will be in enviable positions as this transformation continues. By their very nature, entrepreneurs have already accepted total responsibility for the present and the future.

3. The guiding principles that governed the political organizing structure will become less and less effective. With no new universal organizing structure to fill the void, individuals will need to develop their own.

As it becomes increasingly apparent that traditional structures for the organization of society have lost their usefulness, a natural reaction is concern and even fear. It is likely that domestic tensions will increase in the next few years as electorates make increasing numbers of demands on governments that can no longer deliver on their promises.

> ## "Not in his goals but in his transitions man is great."
> — *Ralph Waldo Emerson*

Gradually, however, people will come to realize that the lack of certainty can work in their favor. The new economic structure offers individuals the opportunity to

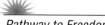
create effective personal organizing structures of their own, ones that make use of — and actualize — their own special talents, passions and missions in life.

Over time, the roles, practices and understandings necessary to the effectiveness of individuals in the new economy are likely to become clear, and this will bring on a period of stability which will mark the conclusion of the Crossover period. In the meantime, this unique point in history — when the structures of society are pliable — presents each of us with unlimited opportunities.

CHAPTER THREE

The Emergence of the Individual

Today's equivalent to *L'Encyclopédie* of Diderot and D'Alembert is the CD ROM of the multi-media personal computer, and our access to the Internet. These tools allow individuals to acquire information from anywhere in the world almost instantaneously, which gives us unprecedented power on the personal level.

> "The entire library of the Sorbonne of fourteenth-century Paris — housing some 2,000 books — could now fit on a few computer disks the size of music CDs, and a few keystrokes could summon any passage from any book in the library."
>
> — *Gregory Stock,*
> *Metaman*

As the individual emerges as an economic force, the time-and-effort gauge of productivity will gradually diminish as a measure of economic value. The key measurements of personal performance in the future will be the results attained through the acquisition of information and the management of knowledge, and through creative innovation in the application of that knowledge.

In an information- and knowledge-based economy, self-confidence will be crucial to individual success. People will come to recognize that it is difficult for those who are functioning within a system established by others to fully develop their self-confidence. Yet the tendency to adapt and become complacent within externally developed organizing structures has been the pattern for most humans for centuries. Many of us are likely to find the transition challenging.

A first and crucial element in the process of building greater self-confidence will be the development by each of us of custom-tailored organizing structures that are suited to our own individual lives. Through establishing our own organizing structures, we can begin to accept the responsibility this transition period has offered us for the moral, social and economic components of our lives. We will begin to think and act in truly entrepreneurial ways.

> "Every man who rises above the common level has received two educations: the first from his teachers; the second, and most important, from himself."
> — *Edward Gibbon*

PART THREE

A NEW FOCUS ON THE INDIVIDUAL

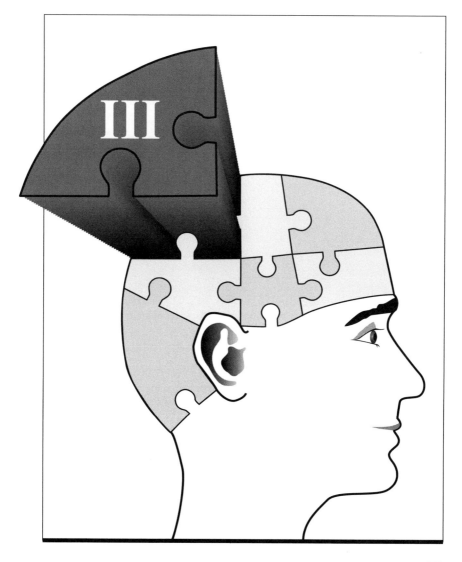

A New Focus on the Individual

The entrepreneurs of yesteryear have much to teach us about managing businesses today. However, the model most of us witnessed most closely as we grew up was not that of the independent entrepreneur, but of the dedicated employee who pursued a single occupation year after year, through thick and thin.

One of the long-term effects of the Industrial Era was that it moved huge numbers of individuals into bureaucracies of one sort or another. Most of our parents and the other adults in our lives were part of this organizational system. It didn't matter whether these people were happy in their work, nor whether they were particularly well suited to it. They believed that if they just kept at it, they — perhaps like their parents before them — would be rewarded. They would receive salaries, raises and benefits throughout their working lives. Down the line, they would receive pensions to see them through their senior years.

Depending on their age, experience may have borne them out; their loyalty and hard work may, in fact, have been rewarded as they imagined it would be. For most of those still in the work force today, however, The Promise of continued employment and a secure future has proven hollow and empty.

Compared to the number of years during which rewards were expected to accrue from dedication and hard work, the current economic structure is new to all of us. However, whether we refer to it as a "job-less" economy or in other ways, it is clear that the conditions that support economic growth today are vastly different from those of any previous generation.

The new economic order presents each of us with the opportunity to develop a working environment that has meaning in relation to our own abilities and talents. Traditional hierarchical structures are being eroded but at the same time, the environment where individual growth and independence can take place is being nurtured. Already we can begin to identify the conditions that will provide the growing medium from which the new entrepreneur — the entrepreneur of the future — can emerge.

C H A P T E R   O N E

Careers, Jobs and Vocations

Even before kindergarten, children talk about becoming nurses, doctors, astronauts or firefighters, and they are encouraged in this direction by their parents and their teachers. What these children are visualizing for their futures, however, often has very little to do with personal interest based on capacity and talent. What these children imagine for themselves — and what they may continue to work toward as they grow toward adulthood — is not a "vocation," but rather a "career" or a "job."

The word "career" shares its root, *carraria*, with a Latin word for "road." A road is all surface. It has been put down to assist people in moving from one place, where the majority is located, to another place — where the majority wants to get. The advantage of a road is that it saves time. Many people are able to make use of it. There is, however, nothing deep or personal about it.

The word "job" is an English expression that refers to a position of employment that requires certain tasks,

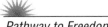

duties and functions to be fulfilled. Jobs have traditionally had nothing to do with the development of individual potential. Quite the contrary. They have allowed humans to be organized for others' purposes — like the cogs of smoothly functioning machines.

Contrast the meaning of the words "career" and "job" with the meaning of the word "vocation." "Vocation" comes from the Latin verb *vocare*, meaning "to call." A "calling," or "vocation," is central and profound. It is closely connected to the inner core of the individual. I cannot practice your calling, and you cannot practice mine.

When we connect with our personal callings, we begin to see our life work as a process in which we are able to actualize our true vocations through the application of our own unique abilities. At this point, we begin the process of unifying our spirit and our work.

When our vocation is realized through our work, our spirit is expressed in our actions and our accomplishments. This leads to greater personal confidence, and to the successful outcomes that result from increased confidence. The value of our work improves in quantum measures, because it is spiritually meaningful.

The concept of a calling presupposes that there is some activity of significance to which we are being called. When we are "called," we know that the time is at hand for us to move forward — to accomplish acts of significance with our lives.

Today, many talented individuals feel they are being called — and, in addition, they feel that their relationship with their existing work is meaningless and frustrating. However, often they cannot see how to align their "calling" with their "work."

Western civilization has socialized us to become "job fillers," rather than "vocation builders," and the educational system has, in large measure, trained us exclusively to fill positions in the work force. Competence has been the benchmark of success, rather than any deep-seated self-confidence in, or commitment to, a life work of our choosing.

Is it any wonder so many of us are dissatisfied? Is it surprising that we thirst for a reconciliation between our spirit of enterprise and the demands of our working lives?

EVALUATING YOUR RELATIONSHIP WITH WORK
Are you a Job Filler or a Vocation Builder?

The answers to these questions may help you begin to determine your vocation.

1. When you were asked as child what you wanted to be when you grew up, what answer were you most likely to give?

_____

_____

2. Was that answer related to a job or career, or to a vocation?

_____

_____

3. List your past source(s) of livelihood on the left side of the page, and your current source(s) of livelihood on the right side of the page.

Past Source(s) of Livelihood	Current Source(s) of Livelihood

4. In each of those occupations in your past, were you pursuing a course that had deep meaning in your life, or were you operating out of a job-filler mentality?

_____

_____

5. Have you ever had the feeling of deep longing or envy when you watched someone else pursue his or her occupation? What was that occupation?

_____

_____

6. Do you see that occupation as a possible vocation for yourself?

_____

_____

7. What aspects of your present work do you love the most? What percentage of your time and effort is spent on those aspects?

_____

_____

8. What would you deeply love to be doing to create a livelihood for yourself?

_____

_____

9. Over the next 90 days, what can you do to make progress towards the vocation or vocational field you've begun to identify?

_____

_____

CHAPTER TWO

The Societal Context for Individual Transformation

❯━┥◆❯━○━❬◆┝━❮

The role of the individual will not change in isolation during this Fourth Great Crossover period, but within the context of societal transformation. Changes to the economic structure of nations around the world are clearly visible today, and these will continue to influence our thinking and our behavior. Each person will ultimately need to assume full responsibility for his or her own economic effectiveness.

Individuals will learn how to motivate themselves, and how to direct their own lives and patterns for learning. By becoming accountable for their own well being, economically, socially and spiritually, they will transform themselves holistically to become truly effective in the emerging economic organizing structure.

Those who choose to become responsible for their own futures during this period of transition will accomplish dramatic advances in the fulfillment of their potential. Three characteristics of the new economic organizing structure will facilitate and reinforce this individual growth and change:

- **Capacity for knowledge**. The individual today is able to acquire information virtually as cheaply and as quickly as any mega-corporation or institution. This gives unrestricted range and potential to all those who are willing to make use of their intellectual capabilities — to all those, in other words, who are willing to focus and be strategic.

- **Economic opportunity**. As we have seen in previous chapters, the traditional, politically based economic models no longer work. This means that the economic playing field is pliable, and each of us has the freedom to create our own small business or other economic structure in order to create the economic results we want.

  Reinforcing this opportunity is the fact that there is less individual pressure to conform to — or vote in favour of — economic polices from traditional leaders that have tended to guide the economic activity of citizens in the past.

- **A conducive environment**. The socioeconomic climate that marks this Crossover period is more intellectually and structurally open to individual initiative than any has been before. As more and more people begin to experience prosperity, confidence, freedom and the other advantages of entrepreneurial initiative, others will observe these working models and stop counting on society to support them. They will begin to examine their own talents and abilities for the creation of personal security. Ultimately, the entrepreneurial approach will become the norm which will, in turn, foster an even more supportive environment for additional initiative.

CHAPTER THREE

The Sovereign Individual

Those who accept that they are responsible and account-able, rather than dependent and entitled, will be empowered by this period in history. They will create their own economic values and their own life structures. In determining the route to the future that is right for them, they will assume in their personal lives the author-ity once held by institutions and political structures. Central to their responsibilities will be the following ele-ments:

- income — how it is earned and how it is spent
- social network and community life
- spiritual exploration and direction
- political involvement and orientation
- education
- health, and health care
- the role of technology, and access to information
- the extent of the influence of outside forces, such as the media

In the past, the direction and control of many of these aspects of life have been the responsibility of political bodies or institutions. Now, each individual has the potential for personal sovereignty.

Autonomous individuals in the new socioeconomic order will establish their sovereignty by drawing up a personal "constitution."

- They will determine their vision and direction for the future.

- By identifying their goals, they will determine their priorities for the investment of time and energy.

- They will become conscious of the values by which they choose to conduct themselves.

- They will develop principles upon which their personal relationships will be built.

The Personal Organizing Structure

Societal organizing structures were created by institutions and political bodies. These organizing structures traditionally dictated what individuals — as members of the community — were to believe, were to perceive and how they were to behave.

By developing the kind of personal "constitution" outlined above, we as individuals today can begin to develop our own *personal organizing structures*. Through our subsequent behavior, we will reinforce or modify our positions in relation to the structures we have developed — and thereby in relation to the world.

With the assistance of individually designed and personally relevant sets of goals and guidelines, we will take responsibility for our lives. We will then truly become "entitled" — to the benefits that accrue to us through personal sovereignty.

The Sovereign Individual

The New Entrepreneur

"Entrepreneurism" is not a new concept, but it is one that has gained new meaning in the evolving economic structure of our times. Individuals who claim sovereignty over their lives and begin to develop organizing structures of their own will be taking the first steps toward the entrepreneurial approach that will spell success — in every sense — in the new economic order.

It is helpful to think of the successful entrepreneur of the future as composed of two separate but closely related elements. The first, the *Inner Entrepreneur* is the internal life which allows us to learn about ourselves, to imagine what we want, and to visualize and then create the opportunities through which we will attain our goals. The *External Entrepreneur* is the outer manifestation of our entrepreneurial spirit, and it is visible in enterprises which create economic value and results.

The energy and spirit of the Inner Entrepreneur direct the External Entrepreneur in every contact we make with the world outside ourselves.

The Inner Entrepreneur

Each individual contains the seeds that are needed to develop a fully actualized Inner Entrepreneur. As we prepare to embrace the new economy, our Inner Entrepreneur will help us to build a personal organizing structure that consistently supports the vision, creativity and strategic process we need to create extraordinary relationships and results.

The Inner Entrepreneur creates the fields where miracles can happen, and makes realities out of dreams. It is the custodian of our greatest ideas, our fiercest passions and our most abiding faith. When confronted with the challenges of the real world, it applies creativity, determination and courage to move us toward our dreams and goals. It is the seat of the human spirit, and the seedbed of great accomplishment.

The Inner Entrepreneur is powerful. It is able to transform us. It can replace old, ineffective attitudes, habits and practices with new and desirable ones. It can free entire personal belief systems, and traditional methods of self-direction and self-evaluation, and lead us into practices that are truly and uniquely effective.

As a bridge builder between dreams and reality, the primary responsibility of the Inner Entrepreneur is the creation of a life structure that allows our individual spirit, genius and ability to shine through. The Inner Entrepreneur works consistently to bring its own spiritual essence, or truth, into concrete form, and it is through the Inner Entrepreneur that we are ultimately able to identify the true vocations of our lives.

The major contribution of the Inner Entrepreneur to our lives is not found in the accomplishment of mere tasks, or in the realization of individual dreams. Its great-

The Inner and the External Entrepreneur: Integrated in Action

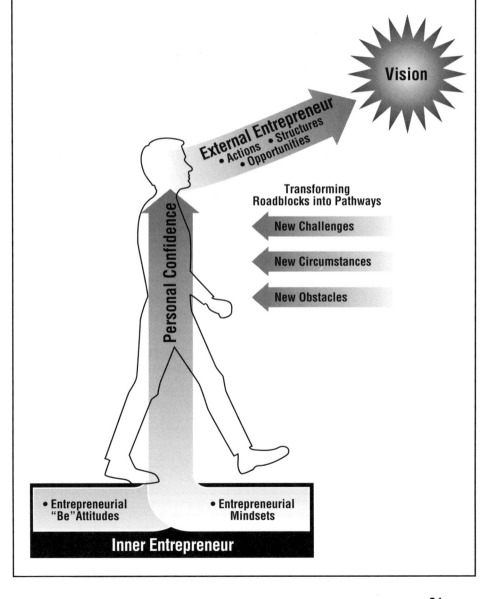

Vision

External Entrepreneur
• Actions • Structures
• Opportunities

Personal Confidence

Transforming
Roadblocks into Pathways

New Challenges

New Circumstances

New Obstacles

• Entrepreneurial
  "Be" Attitudes

• Entrepreneurial
  Mindsets

Inner Entrepreneur

est gift is that it allows us to create holistic, balanced lifestyles while we bring our dreams to life.

The External Entrepreneur

The External Entrepreneur creates the structures that allow our creative ideas to be realized. It brings the vision of the Inner Entrepreneur to life with confidence, and a fully developed set of entrepreneurial skills. The accomplishments of the External Entrepreneur as manifestations of a fully developed Inner Entrepreneur testify to the greatness of the human spirit.

The External Entrepreneur makes optimum use of the range of resources available today on such practical matters as business planning, financial strategizing, and other corporate practicalities. However, the successful entrepreneur lets his or her education, skill acquisition and behaviour be guided from within, rather than externally imposed.

Becoming Entrepreneurial

Individuals in the new economic order will become entrepreneurial in the following ways:

- They will see themselves as being responsible for the integration of all important aspects of their lives — including family function, spiritual direction, social-economic approaches, community involvement and other components — into a personal organizing structure.

- They will develop economic plans that create the best possible blend of unique talents and abilities, economic goals, economic structures, and personal financial objectives.

- They will adopt distinctive economic ways of thinking, and will view their life-long learning process as one that is self-directed.

Noted author and speaker Dan Sullivan expands further on the concept of being entrepreneurial as follows:

> "Successful entrepreneurs differ from other people — not in their abilities, but in their mindsets. They have internalized two fundamental commitments, by making these two decisions:
>
> **Decision 1**. To depend entirely on their own abilities for their financial security (because they realize that the only security is the security they create themselves); and
>
> **Decision 2**. To expect opportunity only by creating value for others (because they understand that this is the only unlimited source of economic opportunity)."
>
> — *Dan Sullivan*
> *The Great Crossover* *(1994)*

In the past, many entrepreneurs focused their time and energy on accelerating their economic results through initiative and creativity. The goal was to create personal security through economic accomplishment, but this often came at the expense of a balanced lifestyle.

Successful entrepreneurs of the future will build holistically sound, balanced and rewarding lives right from the beginning by starting their own personal transformation at the very center of themselves.

CHAPTER FIVE

Attitudes and Strategies

◦—◦—○—◦—◦

While North American society has been supportive of the reemergence of entrepreneurship for several decades, it has not developed a system that fosters the growth of the entrepreneurial spirit.

Our schools do not encourage the kind of independent thought that is necessary for the successful entrepreneur. Instead, they have trained us to conform to traditional structures. Until now, society and the business world in general have reinforced adaptive behavior with approval and tangible rewards.

Today, we must look at ourselves in new ways. We must learn to see ourselves as self-reliant, entrepreneurial individuals with personal talents and gifts that we can contribute to society through healthy, interdependent relationships. We must recognize that we have the inner knowledge that will allow us to reorganize our lives so that the extraordinary individual within us can emerge.

In order to function effectively in a period where we must take full responsibility for ourselves and for our futures, *acting* entrepreneurially is not enough. We must learn to build and cultivate an entrepreneurial spirit and mindset as well. Behavior is the work of the External Entrepreneur; attitudes and beliefs belong to the realm of the Inner Entrepreneur.

Attitudes and beliefs of effective entrepreneurs reinforce the sovereignty of the individual, and therefore generate the most productive behavior on an external level.

- Effective entrepreneurs hold themselves solely responsible for creating their own financial outcomes. They believe that their own talents and abilities will sustain them now and provide them with security in the future. They have released themselves from all vestiges of the "entitlement" mentality that was the legacy of The Promise.

- Effective entrepreneurs do not expect to receive any financial gain until they first create value for others.

- Effective entrepreneurs create economic pathways through their lives that allow them increasing amounts of time and energy for the development and expression of their own unique vocations in the service of others.

Entrepreneurial Spirit Expressed in "Be" Attitudes	Entrepreneurial Spirit Expressed in Mindsets
• Be Personally Responsible • Be Committed • Be Passionate • Be Unique • Be Significant • Be Free	• Visionary • Creative • Strategic • Relationship-oriented

Foundation of Core Values

Defining the Entrepreneurial Spirit's Core Values, "Be" Attitudes and Mindsets

Core Values

Values guide all of our actions to ensure that they are authentic, ethical and consistent with our direction. These are some of the core values that help to form the essential spirit of our beings:

- Honesty, including the willingness to tell the truth;

- Integrity, or the disinclination to pursue a course of action that divides one's mind from one's spirit; and

- Courage, or the willingness to accept risk and fear as experiences, and to move forward in spite of them.

The most important role of these and other core values to the entrepreneurial spirit is that they ensure that we remain as integrated as possible in our relationships with ourselves and with others.

Entrepreneurial "Be" Attitudes

For those new to entrepreneurial thinking, the "Be" Attitudes present a first challenge. They offer us choices about our work. When we choose to incorporate the "Be" Attitudes into our lives, we immediately become entrepreneurial in action through our work.

In the long run, the "Be" Attitudes become constant sources of strength and resilience for us. They serve to remind us of the choices we must make when developing our attitudes towards any particular circumstance connected with our work. We can then use the experience we gain as a source of learning, and as fuel for further advancement along our personal pathway to freedom.

1. Choose to Be Personally Responsible.

We must choose to take responsibility for all of the essential aspects of our lives, including our work, and for the outcomes of our actions.

2. Choose to Be Committed.

We must choose to focus fully on the way we use our time, energy and resources every day, for the purpose of accomplishing our future goals. Choosing to be committed places us in a state of mental alertness, and prepares us to respond to circumstances with action that will lead us — and our team of fellow workers — closer to our visions and our goals.

3. Choose to Be Passionate.

We must choose to believe so strongly in accomplishing a future result that we are willing to transform ourselves in order

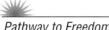
to become better able to reach our goals successfully. Through passion, the spirit of enterprise in each of us is able to anticipate positive change, and to influence the quality of the outcomes of our actions.

4. Choose to Be Unique.

We must choose to be different because we know that progress is possible only if we apply our own unique gifts, talents and abilities to improve our lives and the lives of those around us. If we wish to make a difference in the world, we must begin by accepting the ways in which we differ from others. We must see these differences as strengths, and build our confidence on our own individual ability to make a contribution to the world.

5. Choose to Be Significant.

We must choose to see ourselves as influential and capable of making both modest and great improvements in all areas of our lives — and particularly in our work. We must also choose to engage all of our energy, resources, gifts and abilities in the pursuit of creating the best possible results each time we are called to action. When we choose to be significant, we act differently than we do when we perceive our actions as inconsequential. Choosing to be significant is a personal decision to see our presence and our actions as vehicles by which the lives of others may be improved.

6. Choose to Be Free.

To be free is, in fact, to have the capability to choose, and to be able to act on our choices without constraint. It is to live fully and with a deep sense of appreciation for life, while at the same time nurturing and satisfying our longing for improved results and greater significance and meaning. We must give ourselves permission to dream about the future through youthful eyes, while also engaging all of the wisdom we have accumulated through our experiences. We must guard against complacency, indifference and cynicism, and learn to trust our inner spirit as the true guide of our behaviour, and the source of our being.

Entrepreneurial Mindsets

Mindsets allow us to incorporate our past experiences and our future goals in the interpretation of present circumstances. To the entrepreneur, mindsets are very powerful, as they allow us to recognize the inherent opportunities of any circumstance, and to condition our response to meet the opportunity.

Parts Five and Six of this book explore the following Mindsets, and explain their importance in the development of a truly entrepreneurial approach.

- The Power of Vision
- Creativity
- Being Strategic
- Extraordinary Relationships

Once individuals begin to fully personify the Core Values, "Be" Attitudes and Mindsets of the Entrepreneurial Spirit, they are truly empowered to move forward in their lives and their work.

The Four Essential Strategies

Individuals who wish to develop their own personal pathways through this period of intense and far-reaching change must employ four essential strategies. Each of these strategies is built on the principle that individuals are responsible for creating and directing their own lives.

Strategy 1: Master the central catalyst of change.

As we have seen, the central catalyst of change during this Great Crossover period is economic. This means that each of us must master the economic aspect of our lives before we can effectively integrate all the other significant components of our lives. Consistent growth and fulfillment in other areas of our lives will be supported by mastering this key component. Because of the nature of the questions facing our generation, financial self-reliance will increasingly become an indicator of our commitment to personal responsibility.

Long-term confidence is central to our ability to influence and direct the increasingly complex sets of priorities and responsibilities that our lives will present to us during this period of change. Those who are unable to master the economic aspects of their lives — or choose not to do so — will find it almost impossible to gain this confidence. Feelings of financial insecurity will cause them to remain dependent on the decisions of others regarding their value and their roles.

Strategy 2: Understand The Holistic Nature of Change

While mastering the economic aspect of our lives must be our first priority as society as a whole moves from a political to an economic organizing structure, we must also keep in mind that change is holistic. The whole is found in every part of us, and altering one aspect of our lives will affect all other areas as well.

While it is possible to differentiate the unique components that contribute to the makeup of each individual, in reality it is impossible to separate them. Understanding the holistic quality of human nature is crucial to a complete understanding of the strategies we need in order to be effective.

It is particularly important to remember this truth as we move through this Crossover period. We must attend to all areas of our lives at once when making changes in any one area. We must remember that a decision to develop ourselves as entrepreneurs will affect not only our economic prospects, but also our relationships, our health, and every other element of our lives.

Whether changes come from outside ourselves — as are many being experienced today by those in traditional places of employment — or whether they result from our own decision to take a new direction in the future, it is important that our responses take all aspects of our natures into consideration. We cannot afford to think linearly when it comes to incorporating any major change, whether it is internally or externally imposed.

Fatigue, distraction and fragmentation handicap our ability to achieve self-transformation. Change requires energy, time and focus, and we can easily lose the direction and confidence we need to accommodate it. Particularly given the complexity and intensity of our lives, we must try to remain as balanced as possible while implementing change.

Strategy 3: Put the Entrepreneurial Principle to Work

An entrepreneur takes a resource from one level of productivity or value, to a higher level of productivity or value. The entrepreneur receives a percentage of the increased value in cash, equity or further economic opportunity.

This is the Entrepreneurial Principle.

The word "resource" can refer to raw materials or unfinished goods as it primarily did in the past, or to information, services, finished goods or time. The Entrepreneurial Principle can be effectively applied on both the internal and the external levels.

Regardless of our current economic circumstances, internalizing the Entrepreneurial Principle will move us toward a life of greater freedom, prosperity and creativity. Using the Entrepreneurial Principle as an operating strategy in our daily lives will place us in the best position possible to employ our unique service, support and vocation to raise the value and significance of our lives, and the lives of others.

Strategy 4. Make A Personal Declaration

It is clear that those with traditional "jobs" in industries with bureaucratic structures will continue to experience the effects of downsizing as technological advancement and economic realities lead to the elimination of more and more labor-intensive and managerial positions. Of even greater consequence, however, is the fact that those whose priorities for their use of time and energy are determined by other people will have limited access to the new levels of personal freedom that this Crossover presents.

This Great Crossover demands that each of us declare our commitment to becoming more entrepreneurial in mind, spirit and practice — whether we are employed by others, or by ourselves. Our alternative is to focus on the past, committing ourselves to traditional control structures and societal guidelines that are no longer effective.

> ## "We're all in this alone."
> — *Lily Tomlin*

The personal declaration to move forward entrepreneurially is the first and most significant act the sovereign individual can make. By declaring ourselves true entrepreneurs, we eliminate confusion and fragmentation of responsibility and purpose.

This personal declaration will have lasting power and significance. It will affect the structures we establish for ourselves, the levels of freedom or fear we choose to live with and, ultimately, what we accomplish in our lives. As we determine our own pathway to freedom and prosperity, this declaration will allow us to focus our skills, our vision and our creativity.

The balance of this book discusses the ways in which we can gain the self-confidence we need to shape our futures. By combining these approaches with the four essential strategies, we can tap the power within ourselves to move forward with strength.

UNBLOCKING YOUR PATHWAY TO FREEDOM

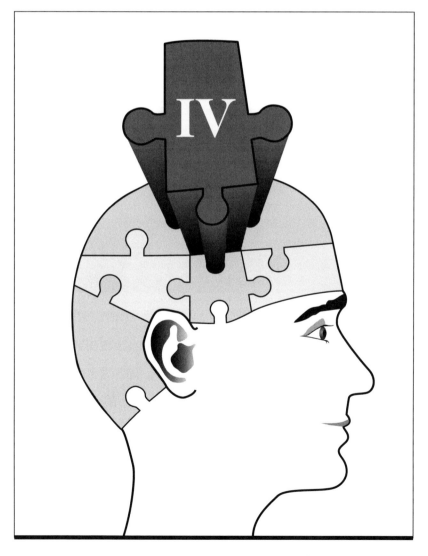

Unblocking Your Pathway to Freedom

In some ways, the mind is like a workbench. Over the years we collect a variety of tools: some we need infrequently, others we make use of every day. From time to time we replace a broken implement, or make a new, high-tech addition to our collection. Because we don't have time to get rid of the tools the new ones were intended to replace, we end up with a disorganized clutter.

Rarely do we take the time to examine the contents of the workbench as a whole, to make certain that the tools are still in good working order, still effective and still useful. As a result, we occasionally reach for one of them, only to find it is no longer suited to the task we want it for.

Over the course of our lives we have accumulated a similar workbench of beliefs and attitudes. Some are carefully honed and ready to be used at any time. Others — and we may even forget we have them — fall into disrepair, become outmoded or outlive their usefulness. Ultimately, rather than helpful instruments, they become impediments to the accomplishment of our goals and dreams.

This section of the book examines a few of the tools in our mental workbench. Many have been acquired, quite legitimately, during the period of our lives that was governed by political organizing structures. Some of these will need to be repaired, or even to be discarded and replaced, as we move into the new economic order.

We need, for example, to examine our relationship with The Promise — a concept which is now useless and out-dated. We need to remind ourselves to focus on the future, rather than the past. If we think of ourselves as job-fillers, we must learn to see ourselves as vocation-builders instead. Most importantly, we need to examine how we deal with fear, as fear can affect the way we manage the opportunities life has to offer us.

By reading this section and working through the exercises, readers will start to clear and dust their mental workbenches in preparation for their personal transformations.

CHAPTER ONE

Your Relationship with The Promise

In the first part of this book, we discussed The Promise that has guided the behavior of several generations of workers. The Promise said that if you worked hard and remained loyal to your employer, you would be rewarded. With governments and organizations no longer in a position to fulfil The Promise, it is time for us to erase it from our thinking processes.

Letting go of the concept of The Promise is not as simple as recognizing its hollowness on a conscious level. It is necessary for each person to examine his or her relationship to it, and to determine the depth and longevity of his or her trust in its "guarantees" for the future. Only by exploring this relationship in the light of today's realities can we begin to let The Promise go.

"I" and "They"

The Promise is very powerful. While it is rarely verbalized, most of us have internalized it. Despite the fact that The Promise comes from no specific place, it has been understood and accepted by almost everyone. Because it is unstated, it is almost hypnotic in its power.

As long as any of us believes that someone or something "out there" is going to provide us with security, we are haunted. We are unable to gain enough personal confidence to be fully effective in today's economic environment, for we are dependent on others. We are dependent on people we cannot even identify.

The Promise erodes personal responsibility. It says, "If you behave in certain ways, 'they' will take care of you." Furthermore, it implies, "If you cannot or will not behave in these ways, 'they' will still take care of you." As a result, we have come to depend on others — invisible others, for the most part — for our security. This way of thinking is political and global. It allows the "they" to become more powerful than the "I." This way of thinking disempowers us.

If we continue to allow The Promise to hold power over us, the organizing structures of others will continue to control our lives. We will feel increasingly frustrated, dissatisfied and overwhelmed, for we know that those traditional organizing structures no longer work.

If, on the other hand, we release our thoughts and attitudes from all vestiges of The Promise, we will take a very important step toward giving ourselves the freedom to develop our own personal organizing structures.

Think carefully about The Promise. How deeply do you believe in it? To what extent do you let it guide the significant areas of your life? Only by letting The Promise go can you begin to assume the total responsibility for your life that can lead you to greater levels of confidence and freedom.

Your Focus — Past or Future?

While learning from the past is an essential part of growth, there are individuals whose focus on the past is so pervasive that it prevents them from moving forward. Only by consistently directing our thoughts towards our goals and dreams can we take the necessary steps in our daily lives to bring our visions to life.

A great deal has been written about the positive relationship that exists between vision and personal transformation. It is important to keep this important relationship in mind as we establish our own personal organizing structures. A personal organizing structure is a roadmap for the future, and when we think about the way things "could have been," or things we "should have done," we are not helping ourselves to implement that structure in our lives.

Unproductive Thinking Patterns

Past-focused individuals tend to long for the past, and to feel betrayed that life is not turning out as they had hoped it would. They spend a lot of time identifying and complaining about the factors that have led to downsizing in the workplace, to betrayals of The Promise and to other current realities. They are quick to lay blame on political leaders, economic forces and technology.

Past-focused individuals tend to be self-righteous and critical of others. On a personal level, they have long memories when it comes to slights and arguments. Their attitudes contribute to family strife, and can act as blockades when it comes to the self-fulfillment of others.

By assigning blame for what has come to pass, these individuals are avoiding responsibility for their lives and for their futures.

Looking Forward

Future-focused individuals have a much more positive approach. They see the world in terms of possibilities and opportunities. They are empowered by their acceptance of full responsibility for their lives and for their futures. By setting goals for themselves that they are eager to attain, they contribute direction, purpose, and optimism to their lives.

People with big futures need a lot of energy, and a well of vitality just naturally seems to deepen in future-focused individuals. Even before they solidify their personal visions or develop comprehensive organizing structures, they are purpose-centered and enthusiastic. Their energy and enthusiasm attract others who also have goals and dreams. They are, in short, stimulating company.

Self Assessment

It is helpful from time to time to ask ourselves the following question: "What do I want to accomplish, both personally and professionally, between today and the same date three years from now?"

If we are focused on the past, we will have no clear idea what our hopes and dreams may be and, if we are able to answer this question at all, we will do so with generalities (I want to be living someplace warm), with unrealistic dreams (I want to win the lottery), or with sarcasm or pessimism (I'll probably be in the poor-house).

If we are focused on the future, on the other hand, we will have given tremendous thought to the future both consciously and subconsciously, and we will be able to answer this question positively, and quite specifically.

No one is entirely future-focused, nor is anyone entirely focused on the past. However, by accepting full responsibility for our lives, we will gradually learn to tip the balance of our thoughts in favour of the future.

In the meantime, we need to keep an eye on our own attitudes and those of the people we know. We need to be aware of the approaches to past and future of other people in our lives, and to be cautious of the influence on us of those who are limited by a past focus. When we find ourselves carried off by a past-focused kind of thought, we need to transform it into a more productive one that is focused on the future.

CHAPTER THREE

Becoming a Vocation Builder

⟫⊶⟨⊹⊙⊹⟩⊶⟨

> **"Where your talents and the world's needs cross, there lies your vocation."**
>
> — *Aristotle*

An individual's true calling integrates the spiritual and material aspects of his or her life and this, at its highest level, is the basis on which successful entrepreneurial enterprise is built.

Identifying a vocation, and beginning to build towards it, is not a simple task: the process can take weeks and even months. However, each one of us does have an individual vocation, and we also have the ability to discover what it is.

Unlike the time-and-effort-based "job-filler" mentality, vocation building involves the element of choice. The

choices it requires are deep and basic. In order to determine our vocations, we must identify our particular gifts and abilities, and then determine how best to put them to use to enrich the lives of others.

Finding our true vocation takes thought and energy, but it is worth the investment. As we develop our vocation-building skills, we no longer feel the world owes us a living. We no longer waste time trying to adapt to the structures of others. Instead, we start to create new structures for ourselves.

We discover that our security for the future lies not in the promises of invisible "theys," but within ourselves and in the relationships we are able to build with others. Gradually — either in the context of the traditional workplace, or by moving toward self-employment — we begin to shift our base of confidence from our competence to fill a job, to our ability to employ our skills and talents in order to bring value to others.

Once we begin to think of the economic component of our lives in terms of a vocation — rather than a job or a career — we can begin to determine how best to use that vocation to meet our economic needs.

Moving Toward Awareness

Although some people seem to be born with an awareness of what they were meant to do in order to create significant lives, most of us are not. We tend to grow into awareness gradually, and with effort. However, this does not mean that we must postpone or avoid the challenges and rewards of becoming entrepreneurial until the vision of our life's work becomes clear.

Some people become frustrated when — after much reflection — they are still unsure about the nature of their vocations. They may give up, and go back to filling jobs. It is necessary to remember that being unclear about one's vocation is not a negative. Uncertainty is a starting point, and becoming aware of one's uncertainty is an important part of the process of developing an entrepreneurial approach.

Learning Through Disqualification

Most often, it is the process of disqualification rather than qualification that moves us to an awareness of our vocations. We begin to gain a sense of who we are by eliminating those life options that we feel are "not right" for us. As we disqualify more and more of these, our confidence in who we are begins to grow. When we put the disqualification process to work in our daily lives, we move steadily toward a greater understanding of ourselves.

When we are presented with a choice, the first step we must take is to "listen" closely to how we feel, and to trust our inner guidance. Through our sense of intuition and discernment, our Inner Entrepreneur will lead us to the right decision.

At times, we will be surprised at the direction we are given: it may seem contrary to all logical and external evidence. The instinct not to take advantage of an opportunity to expand a market, or not to take on an influential new client, or not to accept a position of prestige, may be unexpected and disconcerting. This kind of internal guidance may also make us uncomfortable on an external level, where our need to fit into societal structures is greatest.

Learning to Be True

The "Socratic system of learning", on which our school system was originally based, promoted debate and deliberation in order to expand the understanding of everyone involved. Members of the group used opportunities for dialogue to check their assumptions and modify their conclusions.

The Socratic system served the personal-development needs of students as they learned to be true to themselves. Through the group process, they also came to recognize the value of the ideas and perceptions of others, and experienced the power of the group itself.

Over the years, the school system has gradually shifted its emphasis from encouraging students to be true to themselves, to encouraging them to be "right." In order to be "right," we internalize a long list of "shoulds." Not complying with "shoulds" leads to "mistakes," and we fear making mistakes because they show we are not "right."

However, when we make an effort to be **true** instead of right, "shoulds" are not an issue — and "mistakes" become learning events.

However, through experience we will learn that when an option feels "not right," or when it does not fit within our organizing structures, in the long run the option is worth giving up. Such decisions contribute to, and underscore, our freedom.

By developing entrepreneurial initiatives that honour the inner sense of what is right for each of us — by disqualifying what feels unsuitable — we develop our inner confidence and build our body of experience. At the same time, by improving our sense of what is right through disqualifying those options which are not, we move continually closer to an awareness of what our vocation really is.

Unfamiliar Territory

Disqualification is a difficult process for many of us to employ, because we were not raised to consider it as one of our learning options. In order to create individuals who are able to compete in the employment marketplace, formal learning tends to focus more on competition than on personal development. In addition, society expects us to be competent, confident individuals who consistently have the "right" answers, behave in the "right" manner and pursue the "right" directions. Self-image and self-confidence have become tied to external definitions of what is "right." Disqualification requires us to find out, through experience, what is not.

Disqualification forces us to think of ourselves as learners, rather than as knowers. Knowers may be "right" more often than learners are, but they often lose the ability to be *true*. Learners are able to expand the limits in the search for their individual gifts and talents.

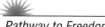
Disqualifying is an honorable way of learning. In addition, it is a characteristically entrepreneurial learning approach because it is based on the truth that absolute answers are, in most cases, illusions.

As the vocation-building process continues, disqualification proves itself an increasingly rich resource. By learning what we are not, we gain direction for our lives and increase our confidence. No matter how long — or how short — the period of focused self-discovery turns out to be, we move continually closer to finding our true vocations.

CHAPTER FOUR

How Do You Deal With Fear?

Those who have depended on the philosophies and guidance of institutions for the development of their own structures and practices in the past — no matter how individually restrictive those philosophies might have been — may find themselves unsettled by the transition to individual responsibility. Unlimited freedom and opportunity can be frightening.

When one accepts individual responsibility and steps toward true individual sovereignty, it is natural to feel fear — to feel as though one has come unanchored.

The Nature of Fear

Everyone is born with two innate fears: the fear of falling and the fear of loud sounds. The entire range of other fears that plague us as human beings are acquired after birth. Even though they are learned responses, they are deep, and they are real — and everyone has them.

The specific nature of learned fears varies from individual to individual. While some of them are physical — fears of bears or lightning, for example — many relate to our behaviour, our daily lives and our efforts at personal transformation. Some fears that can interfere with entrepreneurial development include:

- the fear of the unknown
- the fear of making a mistake
- the fear of being different
- the fear of being successful
- the fear of being powerful
- the fear of what others may think of us
- the fear of following our dreams

PROGRESS

For many, fear presents itself in the form of *resistance*. We find ourselves procrastinating.

- We *do not act on* those matters which will move us forward in our lives.

- We *delay* important vocational decisions.

- We *avoid* making time for our own work.

- We *fail to respond* to crucial opportunities when they arise.

When we find we always have a reason why we cannot move ahead — when something "more important" always lies in the way of our progress — we need to examine our feelings closely. At times like these, we may be facing fear manifested as resistance.

Confronting Fear

It is impossible to "will away" all of our fears. We can, however, learn to use them to achieve our goals. How we manage fear is of ultimate importance. In our weakness, we can find strength.

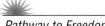

Many would-be vocation builders, vaguely aware that they are afraid of something, will try to alleviate their apprehension by developing good plans and strategies. Although important, good plans are not enough. Only by identifying and facing our fears can we put them to work to transform our inner selves and our external lives.

We must adopt ways of thinking that allow us to become *fear-fueled* rather than *fear-blocked*. What distinguishes the individual who is fear-fueled from the one who is fear-blocked is attitude. Fear-fueled individuals know and acknowledge their fears. They experience them as deeply as they need to. Thus prepared, and with no immediate danger present, *they choose to act despite the fear*, using the energy they gain from transforming fear to fuel their progress and confidence.

Today each one of us is being offered an opportunity for triumph that we could never even have imagined in the past. The future is filled with choices and decisions, and one of the first is this: Do we let fear prevent us from exploring opportunities? Or do we work *with* fear, and move forward?

Fear-fueled individuals have learned from experience that each time they accomplish something in spite of a fear, creativity and energy is released and they gain a new level of confidence. Every fear surmounted is another step toward an autonomous future — another step toward freedom.

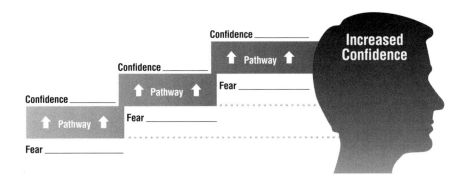

Fear-Fueling Exercise

1. Write down the fear you are experiencing.

2. Identify the new confidence you would gain by acting despite the fear.

3. Develop a pathway strategy by outlining the steps required to transform the fear.

FEAR	NEW CONFIDENCE	PATHWAY STRATEGY
Public speaking: I agreed to be the Master of Ceremonies at my sister's wedding.	I can speak confidently in front of a large group of people.	• Enroll in a public speaking course • Prepare an agenda for the evening • Research and write speaking notes • Rehearse in front of a small group (e.g. family) • Prior to the wedding, visualize myself as the M.C. having fun and speaking confidently • Go for it!

PART FIVE

BUILDING EXTRAORDINARY RELATIONSHIPS

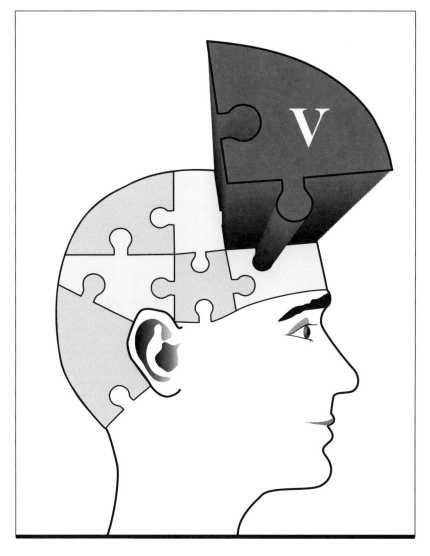

Building Extraordinary Relationships

Self-confidence is crucial to the development of the vision, creativity and strategic process required by today's entrepreneur. When most of us think about how to develop confidence, we tend to think about external mechanisms — going back to school, registering for public-speaking programs, or putting together lists of prospects or sales packages. We know we need to learn how to delegate, how to build teams, how to focus on the money-making process.

While it is indeed necessary to develop our external entrepreneurial skills, we first need to develop that part of the system that supports the vision, creativity and strategic process of our Inner Entrepreneurs. At the centre of that system are the relationships we build — with ourselves, with our life partners, with our business associates, and with other members of our support networks.

While these relationships strengthen and sustain our resolve and our direction, they also serve a secondary but important purpose. They are a training ground for the relationships we need to establish with our fellow workers and our clients. Positive relationships are central to the success of any enterprise, and it goes almost without saying that those who have extraordinary personal relationships will also distinguish themselves in the field of human relations in their business lives.

The Importance of Self-Knowledge

The relationship with the self is the most significant component in building a personal organizing structure that

is right for us as individuals, and yet most people have a very poor relationship with themselves. We can see this lack of harmony in some of those with whom we live and work. The uneasiness we often feel in the company of "driven" individuals, for example, is an extension of the lack of ease that exists between their conscious selves and their spiritual selves. They are working against their inner natures, rather than in harmony with them.

Gaining self-knowledge can be seen first as a process of "involution," during which we explore and confirm within ourselves the core truths and beliefs that define us as individuals. As we deepen our self-knowledge, we are then able to build the necessary confidence to come out of ourselves, into the world and experience. During the "evolution" stage, we can begin to build relationships and structures that will ground us and support our movement forward.

Accounts by those who have been through near-death experiences remind us that as our lives come to an end, what we will consider to have been important will be our relationships. However, it is only on a firm bedrock of self-knowledge that we can learn to let others support our unique gifts and talents with theirs, and begin to contribute support and service to the lives of others in the world.

By making regular use of the Strategic Time Out, we begin to reconnect with our inner selves. During these important periods of solitude, we identify and learn to appreciate our natural abilities, which we can then put to work to benefit our thoughts, our attitudes, and our daily lives.

CHAPTER ONE

The Strategic Time Out

In our usual surroundings, our minds work on automatic pilot a good deal of the time — reacting to the ring of the telephone, planning Sunday dinner, noting that the lawn needs cutting, checking the gas gauge, making lists for groceries. All of us are rooted in routines, and getting away from them from time to time is essential to our health and to our futures.

> **"All miseries derive from not being able to sit quietly in a room alone."**
>
> — *Pascal*

It is also necessary for us to separate ourselves from our surroundings — not only from our normal physical environments, but also from the people in our lives — in order to be able to consider who we are, where we want

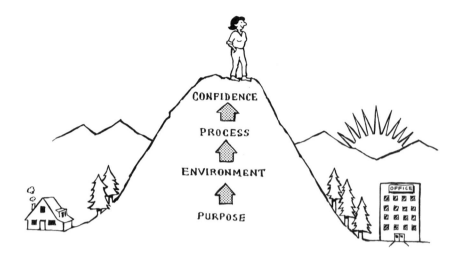

to go, and how we want to get there. We need solitude and quiet to visualize a different future than the one that will unfold if we continue on our present course. We must learn to separate the desired situation from the current one in order to work towards it, and this requires time away, alone.

A "time out" from our daily routine permits our thought processes to slow down enough that we can focus consciously on ourselves and on our futures. During these quiet periods we also learn to measure our reactions to being solitary and alone.

For many, a weekend retreat is a good beginning. Most cities and many rural areas have retreat centres where an individual can go for a few days of quiet and solitary contemplation. Once contact has been firmly established with one's centre, or essential self, the relationship is nurtured and developed by regularly scheduling time to be alone.

Like eating or sleeping, we quickly come to depend on these periods of contemplation for restoration and growth. Those who do not make time to be alone often feel tired and run down. Breaks from daily routine provide the mental rest periods that allow creativity to flourish.

> **"Too exhausted to imagine anything else, most wage warriors simply don't know how to take a vacation.... Caught up in an endless spiral of toil, most of us are our jobs. There is no identity outside the office."**
>
> *—Joe Robinson*
> *Essay on "Vacation Deficit Disorder"*
> *Escape Magazine, Summer, 1995*

The Strategic Time Out

Purpose

To focus consciously on yourself and your future.

To get away from your usual surroundings to consider who you are, where you want to go, and how you're going to get there.

Environment

Choose a quiet place where you can be alone without the distractions of your daily life — a retreat centre, a place in nature where you can camp, or a quiet hotel, for example.

Process

1. Choose your focus for the Strategic Time Out — how you can move from Job Filling to Vocation Building, for example.

2. Book time off — ideally, a full day or more. Organize your support system to allow this to happen.

3. Choose exercises from this book that will direct you during your Strategic Time Out.

4. At intervals during the Time Out, get in touch with your Inner Entrepreneur by taking time for quiet meditation (sitting or walking). Rest, eat well, and enjoy this time to focus on your future.

Confidence

1. Before you finish your Time Out, complete a Strategic Action Plan (see page 184).

2. Schedule another Strategic Time Out for a date within three to four months.

Enjoy your Strategic Time Out. Congratulations on taking a big step towards your big future!

CHAPTER TWO

The Relationship With the Self

> "I had been my whole life a bell, and never knew it until at that moment I was lifted and struck."
>
> — *Annie Dillard*
> *Pilgrim at Tinker Creek*

The Resonance of The Bells

In 1977, bronze bells more than 2400 years old were unearthed in Northern China. These bells were remarkable because each of them had two sweet spots. "Sweet spots" are the notes we hear when bells are rung, and most bells only have one such spot. The two spots on the bronze bells produced two musical tones, one high and one low. When they were sounded together, the result was a deep and satisfying resonance.

Human nature is made up of two components: the external self that we show to the world, and the inner self that contains our essence and our spirit. Like the tones of the bronze bells, these two components are of equal value. One is not better than the other; they are merely different. When these two parts of our nature are working in harmony with one another, their resonance and perfect pitch provide us with the strength to accomplish greatness.

For many of us, however, life experiences have created a gap between the two components of our selves, and they are now working at odds with one another. What has happened is that we have lost touch with our inner selves. When the relationship with the inner self has become fractured, we are unable to move forward. We cannot develop our potential, or find satisfaction in our lives, or contribute our unique talents to the lives of others. We cannot find the resonance.

As we work to become truly effective entrepreneurs, the first relationship we must address, and bring into harmony, is our relationship with our inner self. When we have successfully reestablished contact with the essence of ourselves, and put its knowledge and wisdom to use in our external lives, the two components of our nature will again sound strongly together. Then we will move through the world with balance and confidence.

How We Lose Touch

When we are children and young adults, our families and the educational system teach us the standards by which we are expected to live our lives when we grow older. These standards are repeated so often by the adults we respect that we finally commit them to heart.

The list of expectations we internalize covers a wide range of subjects. It includes the goals we should strive for economically, educationally and socially. It covers lifestyle, family structure, even recreational activities. We learn that it is according to these standards that the world will ultimately measure our success.

> **"The only reason people find their jobs stressful — at least 51% do, according to Gallup surveys — is their lack of understanding who they are."**
>
> *— Sal Divita,*
> *George Washington University,*
> *Washington, D.C.*

As we grow into adults, we transform these expectations into goals of our own. They guide our choices and our commitments, our behavior and our habits, even decisions about where we will live and work.

Living in accordance with certain standards is both necessary and desirable for humans, but when we adhere too strictly to the societal dictates that apply to personal and economic success, we frequently pay a premium. When we strive to attain the goals of others — no matter how much we think these goals have also become our own — too often we relinquish an honest relationship with our own inner selves. We begin to fall out of internal alignment.

When we do try to listen to our selves, the communication lines no longer sing with truth and honesty. Often we lose touch completely with our own goals and desires — if we ever knew what they were. We retreat from discovering or reflecting on them, fearing the price we'll pay in terms of societal approval if we march to our own drummers. We begin to hide our true selves.

And so we carry on, our self-fulfillment deficit growing by the year. Perhaps we tell ourselves we'll get in touch with what we really want to do when we retire, or that we'll devote some time to ourselves during the next vacation. However, we can't fool ourselves forever, and gradually the lack of contact with our own dreams and goals begins to take a toll on our daily lives.

We realize:
- We are not satisfied with the goals we have attained.
- We have no clear vision for the future.
- We feel less capable than we used to.
- We are drained of enthusiasm and energy.

Hitting the Wall

The system for attaining success that we have learned so well may help us meet societal expectations, but it does not give us answers or insights regarding the direction and significance of our lives as individuals. When we feel uneasy in spite of our successes, it means we have not let ourselves grow holistically as we tried to develop our confidence and competence in the world.

People hit their own personal walls at different ages and stages in their lives. What all of us have in common when we reach such points is that we no longer feel capable of moving forward. Our motivation seems to have evaporated. Increasingly aware that life does not last forever, we know that if we are ever going to "make something" of our lives — make a contribution, find fulfillment — we had better get focused. And yet we don't know where to start.

In times like these, we can find reassurance in the experiences of others. From them we learn that our unease is a good sign. Dissatisfaction is a necessary precursor to the process of renewing and rebuilding our lives. Like the wall that marathoners must run through, our wall is invisible and intangible, but it is certainly there. However, with the right approach, like marathoners we can run right through it.

Finding the Way Through

Many of us have been led to believe that certain "experts" have the answers that will solve the problems in our lives. These individuals may point us in the right direction, provide us with food for thought, or give us useful suggestions. However, when we feel dissatisfaction with certain aspects of our lives, we must look within us to find the strength and peace we seek.

The first step in the renewal process is to learn certain core truths about ourselves, including what we believe and what we really want. Only after identifying these core truths can we begin to put them to work in the transformation of our lives.

Making Use of Discernment

It is through the process known as "discernment" that we are able to hear the state of harmony or disharmony between our inner and outer selves. Discernment is most productive during a Strategic Time Out — when we are alone, and ideally in a natural setting. During such times, we can focus entirely on listening to our inner selves, and that helps us to identify the level of resonance between our inner and outer selves. Once we have assessed the state of this relationship, we can begin to re-establish the links between the inner and outer selves that are necessary to move us forward.

The process of strengthening and renewing inner communication is unique to everyone. Where one begins depends on how far out of synchronization the relationship between the inner and outer self has become. Some people are aware only that they are dissatisfied with their lives; they have no idea what they want, or who they want to be. Others know exactly what is making them unhappy, but must learn to tune back into the urgings of the inner self — and learn to trust their intuitions as guidance for the future.

The more adept we become at discernment, the clearer the relationship with our inner self becomes. Honest discernment ultimately brings the inner and outer components of our natures into harmony, providing us with the energy we need for the accomplishment of our goals. The closer to harmony the two parts of our nature are, the greater the energy we are able to tap as we transform ourselves and create new circumstances and opportunities.

Moving Out

Once we begin to know ourselves, we can put our knowledge to powerful use. The valuable insights we gain from our inner selves provide balance to the more rational processes of decision-making. We can begin to make changes to the direction of our lives, and to do so with confidence as we begin to trust ourselves.

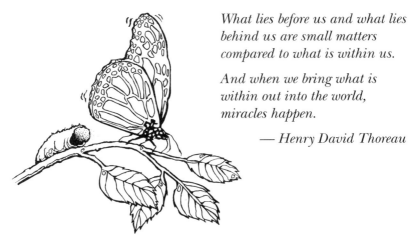

What lies before us and what lies behind us are small matters compared to what is within us.

And when we bring what is within out into the world, miracles happen.

— *Henry David Thoreau*

The more time we spend talking and acting from the foundation of our own core truths, the more we are able to contribute to the world — and the more certain we become that we are, at last, moving in the right direction. When we work in harmony with our inner beings, we reinforce the work we have done in solitude — and we begin to grow even more in our relationships with others.

It is a uniquely human quality to be capable of a relationship with the self. As humans, we have the conscious ability to see life as an observer, a participant and a designer, all at the same time. It is incumbent upon us to make use of this ability.

A healthy, honest relationship with the inner self is a continual source of strength, vision and self-renewal for an entrepreneurial individual. When we are guided by a solid foundation of self-knowledge, we are able to move into the world with confidence and direction. Then the work we do in the external world is in harmony with the true nature of our inner selves, and we gain the resonance of the bells.

CHAPTER THREE

The Power of Two

It is possible for one person alone to create and maintain the necessary energy and stamina to move from one level of personal confidence to another, higher level. However, building a comprehensive support structure — particularly one that includes a life partner in the creative learning environment — will augment efforts beyond imagination. The results produced by the Power of Two in this context are far greater than the combined efforts of one plus one can ever be.

The Power of Two is the energy and vision that is created when life partners reinforce their commitment to one another by:

- sharing their most intimate dreams and aspirations;

- creating together a set of "partnership declarations" that guides their behavior while also respecting their relationship, the other people in their lives, and the pathway each partner has chosen;

- developing a mutual learning process when either or both are moving through transformational life experiences; and

- making important decisions together rather than in isolation.

> **"The only right love is that between couples whose passion leads them both, one through the other, to a higher possession of their being."**
> — *Pierre Teilhard De Chardin*

Taking these steps will accelerate the growth of each partner's personal confidence and effectiveness, while at the same time presenting additional opportunities for cooperative creativity.

Traditional Partnership Models

Entrepreneurs — like those employed by others — have traditionally fulfilled themselves as individuals by focusing their attention and their efforts on their work. Commonly their life partners sacrificed their own needs by putting off the fulfillment of their own dreams and vocations. While the supporting partner was most often female, males have fulfilled this role increasingly in recent years.

The major casualty of this structure is, of course, the supporting partner, who is not encouraged to create and develop his or her own individual vision. Although it is less obvious, the entrepreneurial individual also loses from this arrangement. A relationship in which two partners are growing together and individually provides enrichment not only to the partners as people, but also to the entrepreneurial enterprises in which they are involved.

One of the major drawbacks of traditionally structured life-partner relationships is the low level of actual communication that often characterizes them. When people are operating from traditional structures, the content of many of their conversations and even their tones of voice can sound as though they have been pre-programmed. When genuine dialogue does not exist, partners do not benefit from the vocational and spiritual support of the other. Partners who do not communicate cannot create and explore new vocational pathways together.

The "traditional life-partner" model of relationships is an extension of the job-filler mentality. In our formative years, most of us watched our parents and other significant couples in our lives live out this traditional model. As we grew older, this experience may have influenced our expectations for our own intimate relationships.

While it can be difficult to break away from this traditional model, there could not be a better time to do so. The negative aspects of traditional life-partnership roles are particularly counterproductive to the realization of the kind of fully developed vision that will be appropriate in generating family security in the new economy. Life partners who initiate entrepreneurial ventures together or separately will be handicapped if they attempt to communicate from traditional models.

If they are to be creative, grow and prosper, life partners must not only develop mutually satisfying visions for the future, they must also engage in truthful dialogue regarding such crucial details as family financial objectives and the separate and joint uses of time and energy.

Sharing Core Truths

Life partners do not normally avoid telling one another the truth. Many, however, have great difficulty in sharing such intimate matters as their hopes and dreams, their aspirations for personal accomplishment, and their visions for making their lives significant.

The Power of Two is activated in relationships that are marked by an intimate level of mutual trust and respect, and life partners need to invoke this consciously when it comes to communicating core truths. By doing so, they can renew their individual visions, and at the same time

establish a healthy, productive and creative communication process. By supporting one another, each will gain greater levels of personal confidence and awareness.

First Steps Toward True Partnership

The valuable moments of intimate conversation with our life partners — when we discuss priorities and financial objectives for our lives and our businesses, and when we share visions and dreams about the future — should reflect the content and the honesty of the times when we speak with ourselves. The trust that we place in our life partners when we are committed to communicating core truths often allows us the first verbalization and externalization of creative ideas that previously existed only inside ourselves.

The first step in establishing a viable co-creative communication process is for life partners to assess their relationship objectively. They must determine the current state of the vision and communication process that exists between them.

The Strategic Retreat

Once life partners begin to move away from traditional roles, they can increase the emphasis on true partnership by conducting a Power of Two Strategic Retreat. During this time out, a number of crucial strategic processes can be completed that will lead to greater partnering strength.

After the preliminary retreat, follow-up retreats should be planned to occur every three to six months. Subsequent retreats help partners to stay on track, and allow them to make any necessary modifications to their direction and their plans. It also provides the opportunity for assessment and evaluation, which builds the confidence of both partners in their ability to create and develop big futures together.

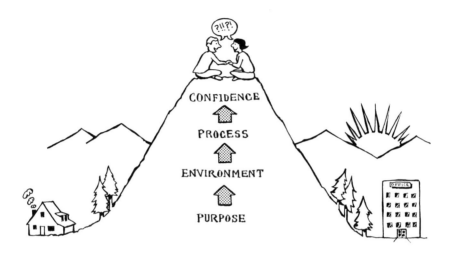

THE POWER OF TWO
Strategic Retreat

The following exercise has been developed to assist partners during Power of Two Strategic Retreats. This exercise will also serve as a valuable tool for an individual Strategic Time Out. When using this exercise for a self-directed retreat, simply respond to each section as an individual.

1. Warm up

Spend some time reviewing your answers to the introduction exercise (page 20) and the Vocation Builder exercise (page 71).

2. Core Truths

One way to begin telling core truths is to state to your partner what you really want in your life. Spend some time sharing your dreams and vision of the future by answering the following question: "Over the next three years, what do I want my life to be like? Consider your —

- Partnership
- Health (physical and emotional)
- Family and Friends
- Career/Vocation
- Finances
- Recreation/Rejuvenation
- Spiritual Direction
- Community
- Other Areas _____

Document your answers to this question, and use this information to formulate a list of goals.

3. Partnership Goals

A. As partners, individually and together, what key goals do we want to achieve over the next three years?

1. _____ 11. _____

2. _____ 12. _____

3. _____ 13. _____

4. _____ 14. _____

5. _____ 15. _____

6. _____ 16. _____

7. _____ 17. _____

8. _____ 18. _____

9. _____ 19. _____

10. _____ 20. _____

B. The most important goals we want to achieve over the next year are:

1. _____ 6. _____

2. _____ 7. _____

3. _____ 8. _____

4. _____ 9. _____

5. _____ 10. _____

4. Three-Month Strategy

Review your three-year goals and one-year goals. Looking at the next *three months*, discuss what progress you can make toward the achievement of your goals. Complete the following plan by listing your three-month goals and the steps required to accomplish them.

Three-Month Action Plan From _____ to _____

Three-Month Goals	Step 1	Step 2	Step 3
1.			
2.			
3.			
4.			
5.			
6.			
7.			
8.			
9.			
10.			

5. Evaluation

Schedule dates to evaluate your progress, celebrate your success and to make any changes to the plan that are required.

Date _____   Date _____

Date _____   Date _____

True Magic

In a true partnership, we will accomplish personal transformation far more quickly than we can ever manage on our own.

A true partnership increases our personal confidence, enabling us to:

- commit ourselves to practicing vision, creativity, relationship-building and being strategic;

- experience major increases in energy and stamina, which in turn allow us to follow our visions through all kinds of circumstances and challenges; and

- follow our vocational callings, wherever they may lead, without fear of loneliness.

Magic is seen in extraordinary events. The results that occur as we share core truths with our life partners are truly magical. "True" communication can create miraculous changes in perception, releasing people from the unhappy limitations of traditional roles and allowing them to be honored and supported in partnership as they pursue their individual life missions and vocational pathways. The benefits of living in true partnership include increased personal confidence and greater happiness.

CHAPTER FOUR

The Personal Support System

Our relationships — with our life partners in particular, but also with other family members, friends, mentors and business associates — form our personal support systems. Some people have more extensive support networks than others. As in most things, the quality is more important than the quantity.

We must be continually aware of the extent to which our personal support systems can affect the fulfillment of our goals. We must also remember that the nature of the support we receive arises from the relationships we choose to have. If relationships hold us back, we must accept responsibility for having let them do so.

Designing a personal support system is a significant step in the development of the entrepreneur. We have all watched people become confused or disillusioned as a result of spending time and emotional energy with people who have negative attitudes. The impact of such individuals can be profound, in some cases actually limiting one's potential for the future.

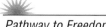
On the other hand, a positive personal support system creates a "vision community" for all of its participants. Its members are sustained by the trust they have placed in one another, and the group becomes a valuable forum in which the core truths of individuals can be explored, understood and put into practice. All successful businesses are built on a foundation of excellent relationships. Developing meaningful and mutually supportive relationships in our personal support system is a crucial step in gaining the confidence to build extraordinary business relationships.

A positive system of interpersonal relationships can help to ensure that our confidence is not severely damaged by the lessons life is sure to teach us. A supportive system can also keep us focused on our progress and helps us to rebalance and redirect ourselves when necessary.

The reinforcement of our support system as we put our entrepreneurial skills to work is far more significant than it may seem. Conversations with members of our interpersonal network are, in essence, conversations with ourselves: they confirm our goals and our direction, and can help to move us forward.

Obviously, it is critical that the members of our support systems be selected with care. Not every relationship — no matter how long-standing or apparently important — is equally positive in moving us toward greater personal fulfillment.

Past- and Future-Focused Relationships

Like individual attitudes, relationships can be classified as focused on the past, or focused on the future. Past-focused relationships can impede our growth; future-focused relationships help to move us forward.

Relationships with past-focused individuals may offer us benefits, depending on who is involved, but they almost always have a negative side as well. Relationships that are past-focused are characterized by critical, narrow and judgmental thinking. As we have seen, past-focused people know how to fix the world, and their vast wisdom is not restricted to global matters. When we tell them about our personal goals and dreams, they are likely to offer warnings and discouragement.

Past-focused relationships can be found among friends, business partners and especially among family members. Based on need, they encourage co-dependence, and they are so common that hundreds of books have been written about dealing with the problems that result from them. We know that these relationships can drain our energy and undermine our confidence, and we need to decide how much time and effort we are willing to invest in them.

A future-focused support system, on the other hand, builds confidence. When based on personal responsibility, accountability and the self-reliance of each individual member, it contributes energy to everyone connected with it.

Future-focused relationships honor the core truths of each participating individual. They create energy that can be used to transform obstacles and lessons into greater insights and opportunities.

These kinds of relationships confirm our direction. When we use our support system as a sounding board, we learn more about who we are, and about what we want. By helping us to ask the right questions, positive relationships also help us to find the answers that are right for us.

Those who have big futures must spend time with other people who are also future-focused. We need to be with our peers — the kinds of people who are striving, like us, to fulfill a vision. We also need to associate with mentors — those who are actually living the kinds of lives we hope to live, in our own unique way, at some point in the future.

Future-focused peers facilitate our learning, rather than impeding it. Future-focused mentors coach us rather than simply instructing us. Future-focused individuals do not believe that they are the experts on how our lives should be lived. They believe we have the answers and the skills within us that we need to help ourselves.

Developing a System that Mutually Supports

A first and important step in beginning to build the support system we truly want is to ask ourselves the following questions:

- What kind of individual would benefit from a relationship with me, and why?

- Am I supportable, and how do I wish to be supported?

- How can I determine the needs that others have for support, so I can support them?

Each of us has gifts and talents which complement those of others. We must remain open to other people, allowing ourselves to be supported and to support others in return.

Transition

It can take weeks or months to transform our own self-image and establish a new direction. During this period, we will begin to recognize that some of the relationships in our lives are positive and others are not. A transition period in our relationships with others often coincides with the period during which we begin to establish a more honest relationship with our inner selves.

As we learn to clarify the picture and tone of our future-focused selves, and envision ourselves as we want to be in the future, we begin to see the roles and support that others fulfill — and can fulfill — in different areas of our lives.

Clearly, we want to develop or maintain relationships with others who are also working towards big futures, and with those who can be mutually supportive of personal transformation. We may even seek out new relationships — by attending seminars, courses or workshops, for example— that reinforce the alignment between who we are today and who we choose to be in the future.

Our own behavior will influence others as well. As we gain a greater sense of who we are and where we are going, our way of relating with others will begin to reflect our own future focus. In some cases, this change in us will serve as a model or a catalyst to others, preparing them to move into personal transformations of their own.

> **"It is one of the most beautiful compensations of this life that no man can sincerely try to help another without helping himself."**
>
> — *Ralph Waldo Emerson*

Forgiveness

The cornerstone of a successful future-focused relationship is the ability to share core truths and beliefs. Releasing ourselves from perceived hurts and wrongs facilitates this honesty, and is a liberating experience.

It is our responsibility to heal ourselves of the negatives that are contained within us. By making use of forgiveness to empty ourselves of bitterness and the critical and judgmental aspects of our nature, we become open to receive new insights that can lead to new growth. We are essentially letting go of one thing in order to be free to receive the spirit of another.

Forgiveness is the first step in our liberation from the invisible hooks of past-focused relationships. If we are willing to be responsible for healing our inner selves of illusions and grievances, life will fill it with vision and renewed faith.

Eternal Friends

Over the course of our lives, many, many people will help us in their own unique ways to make meaningful contributions to the world, and to accomplish the successes we seek. Of that circle, a certain number of individuals will go beyond mere association and friendship to become "eternal friends."

Eternal friends may appear anywhere in our network of mentors, coaches, close friends, parents, spouses and business associates. The support of these special people goes beyond descriptive roles, however, and gradually they attain spiritual significance in our lives.

Eternal friends seem determined that we will achieve our life's mission, and their commitment goes beyond the rational. These individuals tend to show up at crucial times in our lives — when we need to make fundamental choices for the future, for example, or to redefine our attitudes and our approach. They do not exist to do our "work" for us, but are there to listen, and to support.

While eternal friends are, by definition, friendly, they are not always the most sensitive members of our circle of companions. They constantly remind us of our ultimate

personal responsibility, and they demand that we remain true to ourselves.

All of us should occasionally take the time to think about our eternal friends. Where possible, we should make the effort to explain to them — by phone, in person, or by letter — their importance in our lives, and to thank them for their contribution. When this is not possible — some of our eternal friends may no longer be living, but may still contribute tremendous support to us — a few moments of grateful meditation can be a meaningful alternative.

We recognize our eternal friends by instinct and intuition. They are among the greatest blessings of our lives. We often discover — not surprisingly — that we fulfil the same crucial role in their lives as they fulfil in ours.

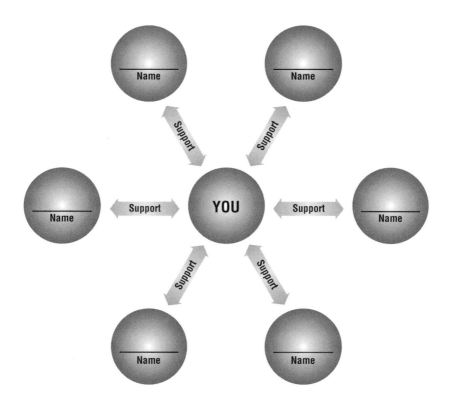

Building a Personal Support System

1. Identify the key people in your personal support system — those people who support you and whom you support. Remember that the *quality* of relationships is more important than the *quantity*.

2. Schedule time to connect with each person and discuss:
   - Your visions for the future.
   - Your progress toward vocation building.
   - How you can support them.
   - How they can support you.

PART SIX

THE PERSONAL ORGANIZING STRUCTURE

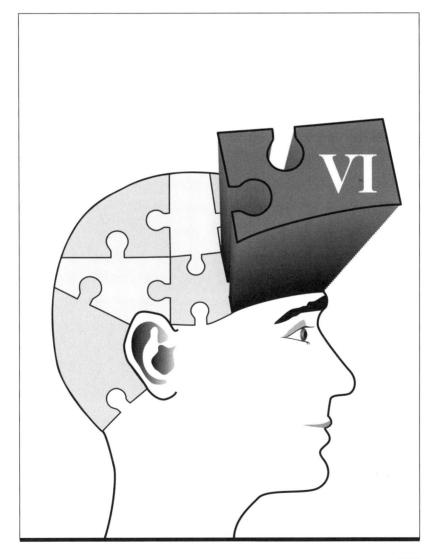

VI

The Personal Organizing Structure

As we have seen, an "organizing structure" is a model of human organization which is based on a specific set of:

- beliefs,
- rules, and
- guidelines for behavior.

As we move toward individual responsibility and decrease our dependence on societal organizing structures, the most important first step we can take is to assume authority for ourselves. We can do this by developing a personal organizing structure that will ultimately allow us to discover and fulfil our true vocation.

We have also seen that economic and political conditions make this an ideal time for entrepreneurial initiative, and technology allows us to become successful as entrepreneurs by providing each of us with immediate access to the information networks we need. In order to take full advantage of this environment, each of us must develop a framework which will allow us to put our particular abilities and gifts to optimum use.

While a societal organizing structure is designed, dictated and enforced by religious, political or other societal systems, a personal organizing structure is designed, dictated and enforced by the individual.

By working toward his or her goals in the context of a personal organizing structure, each person is able to:

- let go of The Promise of societal salvation by assuming complete accountability for his or her individual security — economically and in all other ways;

- accept responsibility for becoming a Vocation Builder;

- initiate a process of lifelong learning that makes full use of all relevant sources of information and knowledge available today; and

- create value for others by practising the Entrepreneurial Principle — in all economic and significant personal activities — thereby contributing to the community as a whole.

With the assistance of a personal organizing structure, the individual's activities, educational processes and lifestyle support his or her long-range goals and objectives. The structure supports the individual's efforts to move toward greater levels of personal life-significance, and greater levels of personal freedom.

Personal organizing structures are not static. Individuals who choose personal transformation during this Great Crossover period will continue to modify their organizing structures over time, incorporating new processes that will make their lives increasingly effective.

In order to develop a personal organizing structure, we must develop three essential resources that are within each of us — creativity, vision, and the ability to be strategic. Understanding our relationship with risk will allow us to put these resources to their most effective use.

CHAPTER ONE

A New Encounter With Creativity

Creativity is a powerful ally. It is the pathway through to our successful selves. It allows us to transform ourselves and our circumstances, and it guides us in the choice and development of our vocations.

The importance of developing a fully creative self cannot be overstated. Creativity creates more creativity. Without it, we cannot change.

The creative self is one of the most important components of the inner being that defines each one of us.

What is Your Relationship with Creativity?

Most people do not have a positive relationship with creativity. They use such adjectives as "haunting," and even "painful," to describe their association with this aspect of their inner selves. Until they begin to see the potential of their own creative abilities, they rarely associate them with such words as "joyous" and "empowering."

Many individuals grow angry when they think about their own creativity. They are not angry with themselves per se but probably with the life experiences that have caused them to stifle their creative selves. They may feel anger with the immediate environments in which they find themselves, or with their parents, teachers and others in the past, or with society in general, or with the universe and the way it functions.

"I was born with such talents!" they think, shaking their fists at the heavens. "Why wasn't the world structured so that I could easily make use of them?"

For most people, the creative experience has not been the day-to-day reality of adult life. The anger they feel as a result is real and justified. It is caused by the loss they have experienced — not only of creativity, but also of the kind of energy that only creativity can release.

It is not only those working in traditional kinds of employment who find themselves blocked creatively. Many people we might consider to be involved in highly creative endeavors are also unable to make use of this aspect of themselves — the visual artist, for example, who works in a graphics-design firm and "never has the time" for her own creative work, or the orchestra's cellist, who believes his musical agenda has been decided by someone else.

When a person feels creatively stifled, it is often because he or she is conforming to someone else's organizing structure and is, in the meantime, moving no closer to the achievement of his or her own life's work.

Rather than taking responsibility for their own futures, people who are so afflicted often blame their circumstance on forces outside themselves. They wait for someone outside of them to provide them with an environment that will allow their creativity to flourish. They may actually think that it is the world's responsibility to create an organizing structure for them, so that their creativity can emerge.

These people often feel that they are "entitled" to a certain way of life, and that circumstances have betrayed them. They are angry because it appears that the world does not function in such a way that they can find fulfillment — in other words, that it was not created with their needs in mind.

Obviously it is true that the world was not created for any particular individual. However, the fault is not in the world, but in the way these people see it. Rather than being stifled creatively by outside forces as they believe they are, these individuals are actually withholding their creativity. They are probably doing so unconsciously, perhaps as a result of deep-seated fears that are associated with changing their approach to a more creative one.

But the truth is that their creativity has not been entirely blocked. They have created their own world, their own reality. Furthermore, they have a magnificent opportunity if they choose to act on it — they can create another reality for themselves.

How Creativity Gets Blocked

By nature, children are creative. As they learn about the environment that surrounds them, they invent explanations for the occurrences they see that defy all adult "logic." Children devise imaginative ways of dealing with the world that sometimes delight and occasionally alarm their parents and their teachers.

All of us were creative when we were children. Whether we continue to be creative in adulthood depends in large measure on the feedback we received for imaginative thinking and behavior when we were young.

Any chinks in our confidence in our creativity were likely put there by the authority figures of our childhood — parents, teachers, religious instructors, or other adults. When our childhood creativity is discouraged, we learn that creativity is of little value. If we are taught to conform to existing structures, we never learn the power of creating our own structures. As a result, too many of us end up in dead-end careers with deep-seated longings for lives and vocations that are purposeful and meaningful — and also fully creative.

> ### "The great man is he who does not lose his child's heart."
> — *Mencius*

Apprehension is common in adults today when it comes to creative expression. Unless we take steps to address the fears associated with creativity — by allowing them to fuel us, rather than to block us — the negative feedback we have received in our early lives will affect our ability to use creativity to change and improve our lives.

The Nature of Creativity

Before we can fully tap into the power and energy creativity can offer us, it is necessary to recognize that it has not one form, but two.

Creativity is not, as most people think, solely restricted to the world of self expression and artistic enterprise. Nor is its role in the business world exclusive to such areas as product development, advertising and promotion. While a creative approach is central to success in these and many other areas, creativity is also essential in the development of our individual selves — and our lives.

Self-expression, the form of creativity with which most of us are familiar, allows us to *respond effectively to creative opportunities in specific circumstances* — by finding innovative solutions to business problems, for example, or by creating music or art. This form of creativity is the externalization of our unique talents and our "essence." Developing this kind of creativity is important, and tapping it can provide us with deep pleasure and energy. However, self-expression is only one component of creativity.

Creativity also allows us to create our *life circumstances and our personal organizing structures.* This form of creativity allows us to determine who we are, where we want to go, and how we want to get there. It allows us to transform roadblocks into pathways, and to create the necessary structures for personal fulfillment. The personal organizing structures that we create with this kind of creativity will provide a context for our creative activity in the future.

The truly entrepreneurial individual integrates the use of creativity on both of these levels.

The characteristics of integrated creativity are as follows:

Creativity provides energy. The energy provided by creativity is different from energy generated in any other way. When creativity is at work, we no longer function in "survival" mode — merely getting through the day.

Instead we feel energetic, inspired and spurred onward to develop and explore our selves and our futures.

Creativity provides security. When we make use of creativity to fulfil the potential of our own vocations, we gain tremendous security in our own abilities and talents. Instead of fearing that we may lose what we have gained, we are able to look at what we have created, and know we can do it again — at any time, and in any place — and probably do it faster. Our creative abilities are unique to us, and as we link their use with the Entrepreneurial Principle, they ultimately become our security.

Creativity provides confidence. As we begin to recognize the security our creativity gives us, we gain tremendous confidence. We work continually to overcome any fears

INTEGRATED CREATIVITY

that block our creativity, and each time we are successful, our confidence is boosted. Increased confidence allows us to take risks, to take advantage of essential opportunities, to make difficult decisions, and to create the organizing structures that allow our lives and our vocations to be fulfilled.

Creativity unifies. Creative living allows the unification of the self with others. Fully creative people allow themselves to be supported, and they support others. They attract other creative individuals and work together in *co-creative* relationships. The power of this co-creativity contributes to true teamwork, where the essential talents and gifts of each individual work together to accomplish results that are far greater than any individual could ever have achieved alone. It is true that the world was not created for us. Instead, we are here to help create the world. To do so, each of us must *create our own opportunities for creativity*.

We know instinctively that it is unnatural to suppress our individuality and our ability to be creative. We remember — perhaps vaguely, but it is there if we pause to think about it — the energy and enthusiasm that accompanied creative endeavours in our childhood and our youth. The creative self may seem to have disappeared as the years progressed, but it has not. We can re-establish contact — and move forward into a future that is filled with potential for success.

We were all born with unique talents and gifts that have value. We are here to contribute our creative qualities to the world for our own benefit and the benefit of others. Once we see the world from this perspective, we can begin to see how important it is for us to begin the most important "work" of all: creating and living a life of significance.

The Power of Vision

Vision is the ability to see one's desires for the future as though they were already fully realized. By engaging the power of vision, we establish a "magnetic field" that draws us forward with energy and direction. Vision allows us to navigate purposefully through our present circumstances, no matter how difficult and confusing they may sometimes be. With vision, we can see daily events in the context of our goals — and understand that they are part of the path we will take to reach them.

As soon as individuals declare that they wish to live lives of greater significance, they begin automatically to choose to better themselves at every moment — which often leads them into major personal and professional transformation.

Facing the Challenge

Finding our own vision and choosing a self-directed future is not an easy process. Choosing to live a life of increased significance, guided by the spirit of our own personal vision, is to choose to live a life that is never fully defined, and is therefore always growing and changing. Even contemplating such a process can rattle the comfort zones of many of us, testing our willingness to experience "discomfort" for the purpose of greater personal growth and freedom.

> **"Vision without action is merely a dream.**
> **Action without vision just passes the time.**
> **Vision with action can change the world."**
>
> — *Joel Barker,*
> *author, speaker, film maker,*
> *The Power of Vision*

However, those who choose to face the challenges involved in seeking a personal vision and moving toward its fulfillment, will find themselves immediately focused on the future. As they move toward the goals they have established for themselves, they will find themselves grounded and, at the same time, filled with hope and purpose.

Those who choose to live lives that are focused on the future must have faith. They must believe that the deep concerns they have about their present lives are more likely to be answered by creating and directing their own futures, than by continuing to adapt to the patterns of the past.

The Nature and Uses of Vision

Simply put, vision is to the soul what reason is to the mind. Our ability to envision provides us with some of the deepest and most enduring experiences in life.

And yet for many of us, experiences with vision are the exception rather than the rule. While we may call upon this gift in crisis situations, we rarely do so in the context of our routine lives. And yet a lack of vision for the future can cause us to engage in reactive behavior, and make us feel rootless and unfocused.

Vision ensures our mental and spiritual well being. It is as essential to our health as is diet, exercise and sleep. The spirit of vision is as much a part of the unique collage that makes us individuals as is any of our beliefs and habits, and a lack of it limits the human spirit.

Vision keeps us focused on our potential for the future.

We discover our vision by searching for meaning and purpose in our lives. When we face ourselves with honesty, we are reminded of our yearning to live lives of significance. Vision guides us as we move toward a more fulfilling future, and supports us as we create the circumstances that will allow that future to materialize. An effective use of vision provides us with the power to reach our goals, and to eventually become the person we aspire to be.

Vision leads to major breakthroughs in learning.

Vision provides us with a context for learning. It allows us to choose to view the lessons life offers us as learning experiences from the perspective of our future selves. It shows us that there are no mistakes or failures — only opportunities to learn. This attitude is a powerful ally as we navigate through life.

A solid vision for the future also gives us faith in our own abilities as learners, and confidence in the integrity of the learning process itself. As a result, we are able to suspend our need to be "right" long enough for a new view or a new result to reveal itself to us. Vision, in this sense, supports us as we focus on developing creative strategies, rather than relying on outdated and ineffective ones.

Vision revitalizes us. It supplies us with confidence and hope.

> "Those of us who made it through had something significant yet to do in our future.... It is a peculiarity of man that he can only live by looking to the future... and this is his salvation in the most difficult moments of his existence."
>
> — *Victor Frankl, <u>Man's Search For Meaning</u>*

Victor Frankl attributed his survival of the World War Two German concentration camps, at least in part, to his decision to view his experiences in terms of his future self. He applied the hope for his future circumstances as leverage against the hopelessness of his present circumstances, in order to survive long enough for his situation to change.

While most of us will never face the horrors experienced by Frankl, we can learn from his observations about human nature. Vision gives us the power, and therefore the responsibility, to decide our attitudes toward any given situation. When we encounter difficult and challenging circumstances, the power of vision allows us to focus on our future best, and provides us with the hope we need to endure the present circumstances until the momentum turns in our favor.

Vision gives us the focus to transform ourselves.

Individuals who choose to increase the value and significance of their lives must first deal with an accumulation of past knowledge, attitudes, skills and habits — many of which can act as handicaps to growth. The 350,000 hours of conscious and sub-conscious mental programming of an individual who is forty years of age takes on an enormous momentum of its own. The only way to redirect this momentum is to engage the power of vision. By making a personal declaration, and following up with effort and perseverance, we gain the energy and persistence to prepare ourselves for a better future.

A vision of the future is a powerful motivator for change. As our individual visions become clearer, we begin to identify the knowledge, attitudes, skills and habits we will need in order for that vision to be fulfilled. In this way, we begin "re-making" ourselves by developing strategies that are in line with our ultimate goals.

In addition, by establishing a vision for the future — and reminding ourselves of it regularly — we are able to audit, direct and harness our own subconscious minds. In this way, we put to work the powerful resource of mental reinforcement.

Vision gives us the ability to connect with our own personal LORAN system.

The LORAN C system — LORAN stands for LOng-RAnge Navigation — is a tool that allows pilots of airplanes and ships to pinpoint their present locations relative to their points of departure and their desired destinations. Through the use of ground beacons, LORAN constantly feeds back important information such as current location, distance traveled, distance yet to travel, and speed.

The LORAN system provides pilots with a picture that includes the past, the present and the future. They use this information to decide the best strategy to get them to their destinations.

Each one of us has our own personal LORAN system. It can provide us with valuable insights regarding: our past accomplishments; our levels of confidence, knowledge and understanding; the status of our relationships; the best uses of our energy and time; and — to some degree — the time that is remaining to us.

The greatest benefit of our personal LORAN system, however, is that it allows us to be honest and truthful with ourselves — and with others — by discerning the decisions, directions and changes that are right for us. It serves as an internal positioning device that indicates whether or not we are on track and, as such, it allows us to hear echoes of truth or falseness when we check assumptions relating to the future. If an opportunity will lead to progress, we will feel we have the time and ener-

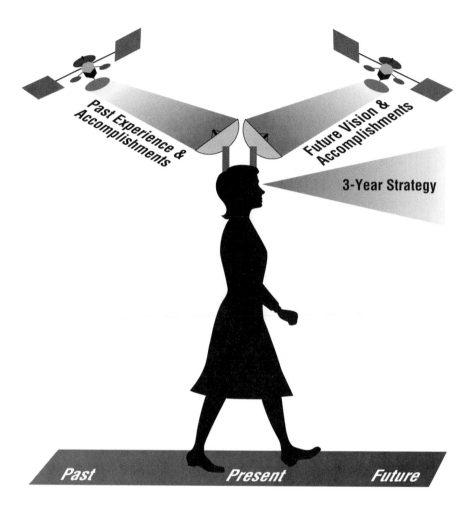

gy to take advantage of it; if it is not the right moment —
or the right opportunity — we will not feel that way. We
must listen to ourselves.

As we become increasingly certain of our true vocation,
our vision provides us with a context that allows us to
interpret the past, and to see the usefulness of our past
experiences. It allows us to make correct choices in the
present. It also provides us with the necessary context —
including the economic context — that will move us
toward the future.

Vision adds value to our relationships with others.

Not every existing relationship is improved by the power of vision. Each of us can name individuals who will feel threatened by our new direction and our growing record of accomplishments. Fortunately, however, by engaging the power of vision in our lives — and by recognizing its importance in the lives of others — the vast majority of our relationships will be improved.

When we believe that others have "big futures" as we do, they learn to trust us and to count on our support. We learn to recognize and to benefit from the unique talents and abilities of one another. We assist one another as we find our places in the world.

With the support of others who are also seeking to realize their own visions, the need to be "right" or to be "good at everything" for the sake of others is diminished. We do not need to compete with those who we recognize and honor.

Flexing The Vision Muscle

As children so often remind us, the ability to visualize is innate. While it has been years since many adults have given themselves permission to flex their imaginative muscles, humans of all ages remain wonderfully capable of doing so.

The ability to make use of vision is linked to a mental muscle that requires regular use if it is to remain in top form. The more regularly we use it, the more clear and precise our visions become. A well-exercised "vision muscle" allows us to maintain overall direction in increasingly complex circumstances. With a little practice, we can recapture and enhance our ability to

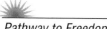

visualize, and we can put this talent to use in extraordinary ways.

Individuals with vision have a very different relationship with time than do those who live without it. A visionary view of the world allows us to live completely in the moment by providing context, which leads to greater understanding. This allows us to respond effectively while enjoying the moment to the fullest.

When we know where we are going, we can stop worrying about the future. We can stop mourning the past. We can focus on the present, and create value in each moment.

Vision and the Entrepreneur

While vision acts like a beacon to the External Entrepreneur, guiding day-to-day and long-term business strategies, it is on the Inner Entrepreneur that it has its greatest impact. It is through vision that the Inner Entrepreneur is able to recognize its essential nature, and to define its goals.

Vision allows us to view our present circumstances as if they were already of the past, thereby creating a temporary bridge in time that allows us to see ourselves at our future best, as though we had already attained it.

When we see ourselves in this way, we essentially create a role model of ourselves. In addition, by anticipating circumstances we may encounter in the future and strategizing how we will deal with them, we begin to build pathways between our present conditions and the destinies we want.

The successful entrepreneur applies vision in two ways —
by putting it to *strategic* use, and by using it to *focus.*

In the *strategic* use of vision, we develop a mental picture
of what we sense is the best pathway to the outcome we
desire. We use the strategic approach to accomplish
desired results. Strategic visions usually focus on issues
that surround "the big picture," and involve determining
the best route to the best outcome for the questions we
are contemplating. Believing that you can reach the
peak of a great mountain, and then committing yourself
to climb it by declaring your intention to do so, would
represent a strategic use of vision. All decision-making
and use of available resources would then be viewed in
the context of this great vision. In this way, vision
becomes a guiding perspective for all activities connected with its accomplishment.

In the *focusing* use of vision, we preview the process for completion of a particular task or set of tasks, while at the same time focusing on the desired outcome of the task. This use of vision is usually practiced prior to beginning the task or tasks, and is like a mental dress-rehearsal that includes the context, the necessary actions, and the desired results of the activity. The focusing aspect of vision allows us to be aware of the circumstances surrounding a task and to continue to work toward the desired outcome. We are able to become so focused on the task that we become one with it.

> **To fly is not to attempt to leave the ground, but to believe that one has always flown, and merely touched the ground to know the sky better.**
>
> — *Patrick Duffy*

The mountain climber described in the previous example might make use of the focusing use of vision to meditate briefly prior to climbing a particular section of the mountain. During this meditation, he or she would visualize the order and successful completion of tasks that were needed to accomplish the climb.

Vision allows us to experience greater awareness, to tolerate new views, and to enjoy new levels of confidence. When we believe in ourselves, we are able to support others by saying "I believe in you," and thereby to inspire them to try a new approach or take on a new challenge. When our approach to life is guided by our vision and focused on the future, we gain confidence. We begin to see ourselves — and our relationship with the world — with greater hope and meaning.

CHAPTER THREE

Being Strategic

What is your experience with setting goals? What is your relationship with planning?

Many people associate these kinds of activities with fear and failure, with broken resolutions and disappointing outcomes. As a result, they are haunted by the very thought of developing — much less undertaking — yet another plan.

However, creating a plan of action — and then carrying it out — is the only way we can possibly transform our lives and attain our visions. Many people have great dreams, but unless there is a process for making these dreams reality, they will lead to nothing.

Successful implementation of a big dream depends on one's attitude toward the planning process. If the attitude is blocked by fear, the process cannot function.

This concept is not new. Over the past few years, hundreds of courses have been taught and hundreds of

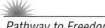
books have been written that address motivational problems. Most people who try to implement the solutions these books suggest soon put them — and their own dreams — back on the shelf.

There is no mystery to the fact that motivational speakers and writers have little long-term effect on the accomplishment of most individual goals. Motivation must arise from within; it cannot be given to you. The fear that blocks accomplishment is also internal, and no one can take it away.

Being Strategic

Bringing a vision to reality requires a strategizing process. "Strategic planning and thinking" — also popular discussion and workshop topics these days — form only one part of this process. In order to bring one's dreams to life, one must not only *think* strategically, one must actually *be* strategic.

Becoming strategic allows us to make maximum use of our limited resources — time, energy, money, and the guidance and feedback we receive from our significant relationships — to achieve our goals. Being strategic allows us not only to develop a clear commitment to the achievements we desire, but also provides us with the opportunity to consider in detail how we will accomplish our goals, and to anticipate problems that may arise.

There are four components to the strategic process:

- Discernment
- Planning
- Action
- Evaluation

Discernment and planning are undertaken by the Inner Entrepreneur, and are manifested in action by the External Entrepreneur. Ongoing evaluation of our strategic processes, and the results they have allowed us to attain, provides us with feedback so that we can make any necessary adjustments to our practices — or, sometimes, to the vision itself — to better meet our needs.

Strategic Discernment

Discernment is a necessary precursor to decision-making. To be discerning involves making use of intuition — which means paying close attention to our own reactions in any given situation, and then trusting those reactions. Our powers of discernment allow us to connect intimately with the heart of the daily tasks that face us, and to sense the courses of action that are right for us.

It can be very difficult to get in touch with our own inner wisdom, particularly when we are surrounded by all of the distractions of our normal daily lives. As a result, many people do not hear or learn to trust the guidance they receive from within themselves, and they end up looking to others for direction. Learning to listen to ourselves requires time and practice, and the entrepreneurial individual needs to spend time alone in order to get in touch with his or her inner wisdom, and to learn to trust it.

Discernment is a way of evoking feedback from our innermost selves. By practising focusing exercises in quiet and solitude, we provide ourselves with the tools that allow us to remain in touch with our own wisdom, and to make the right choices even in the midst of busy, pressured situations.

When we become skillful at discernment, at any moment we are able to ask ourselves what step we should take next, and "feel" the answer that is correct for us. Some people experience this feedback physically — they sense a lifting of the heart, goose bumps, or a "gut reaction." For others, the feeling is not so much physical as mental and spiritual — it is a sense of simply "knowing" deep down inside what is right.

Our vision is for the future, but we can only attain it in the present — real moment by real moment. Those who live exclusively in the future cannot invest in the detailed, minute-by-minute thinking and activity that will ultimately allow their goals to be realized. To develop our talents in discernment, we must learn to move our focus from our long-term vision and to concentrate fully on the present moment. As we do this, our vision will remain within us, and will continue to draw us forward.

Courage and confidence are often required for this shift in mental focus. Only by believing strongly in our vision and ourselves will we be able to successfully commit ourselves to staying on the pathway that will take us to our goals.

Planning

When we have made use of our discernment skills to determine the next best next course of action, we must then employ our creativity to plan its execution. Through effective planning, we begin to move from the internal to the external — and our lives begin to fall into place. Without it, our lives are less focused and our progress not as clear.

Through effective planning, we formalize the strategic process, providing it with structure. The planning process also serves a second, related function — it allows us to face and close the gap that creates a stopping block to the visions and dreams of so many people.

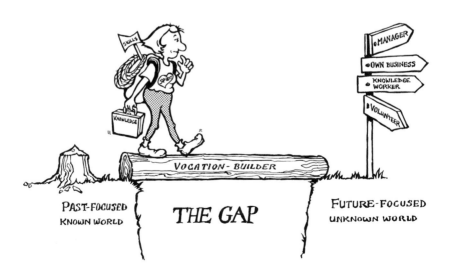

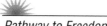
The "gap" is the time that must occur between the present moment and the moment when our vision will become reality. This period of time can seem so long that it becomes a vast chasm into which we fear to step. Contemplating this space can actually stop us in our tracks — and prevent us from attaining our goals and dreams.

In reality, the gap is not nearly as big as we fear it will be — nor is the risk as great. With planning, we can cross this period of time by implementing one small change after another. By taking small strategic steps, we create extraordinary results that move us consistently closer to the realization of our visions.

Although most humans think that they want what they want right now, there is an advantage to the fact that it takes time to cross the gap. We make use of that time to gain our confidence, practise our creativity and develop our organizing structures. These are the tools that we will need as successful entrepreneurs who are in control of our direction and our future. We need time, too, to maintain contact with our inner selves — to learn how to focus and stay calm.

If we examine the records of individuals who have won large lotteries, we see the potentially destructive results of overnight "success." True success comes gradually — and we can make use of the space in time while our visions are developing to transform ourselves as individuals who are ready to embrace what we have created for ourselves.

Plans of action are most effectively developed during periods of solitude. They should be made up of small steps. The sample action-planning form on page 184 can be used to accomplish the simplest task, such as planning a garden, to the most complex — a move, for example, from a "job" to a new self-directed business.

Each entrepreneur must choose the planning system that is most useful to him or her. While both short- and long-range plans are essential to the success of the goal-setting process, the actual nature of the selected planning system is less important than the accomplishment of it.

Action

Taking steps to move through "the gap" constitutes a turning point for the entrepreneur. It is at this point that the Inner Entrepreneur begins to be truly effective in the real world, thereby transforming the external self as well.

When we face the gap between now and our envisioned future, we acknowledge that we are about to place ourselves at risk. As we externalize our vision, we will publicly announce — to ourselves as well as others — that we can no longer continue on the path where life would otherwise have taken us.

It is natural to feel some fear at this point. We must put that fear to use, allowing it to drive us forward into action rather than allowing it to block us, as it may have done in the past. The fear of risk — particularly of the risk associated with crossing the gap — is discussed more fully in the next chapter. In the meantime, we must learn to become "fear-fueled," rather than "fear-blocked." We must remember that by beginning to implement our plans, we begin to move forward — and that our strength and momentum will increase with time.

Strategic Action Plan

Goal: _____

Completion Time Frame

From _____

To _____

STEPS REQUIRED TO ACCOMPLISH GOAL	COMPLETION DATE		RESOURCES REQUIRED	PROGRESS EVALUATION
	PROJECTED	ACTUAL		
1.				
2.				
3.				
4.				
5.				
6.				
7.				
8.				

Evaluation

As strategic beings, we move from discernment to planning, to action, and then to evaluation. The primary goal of evaluation is to build the confidence that will generate the continuing momentum we need to attain our long-term goals. There are four important components to an effective evaluation process.

1. **Establish clear measurements of progress.** The evaluation should include particular landmarks that indicate progress toward the accomplishment of detailed goals. It is worthwhile to identify these key measurements in advance of implementing action.

   If, for example, an individual determines that she needs to be in better physical condition to meet the entrepreneurial challenges ahead, she might determine to work out three times every week and to get a full eight hours' sleep at least five nights a week. Her long-term goal might be to lower her resting heart-rate over a period of six months, and in the meantime she could use graphs to record the successful accomplishment of her weekly, short-term goals.

2. **Obtain feedback from others.** We need to establish mechanisms that will allow us to discuss our experiences and our progress as we implement our plans. This communication is most effective when it is carried out with our life partners, our business partners and/or other members of our personal support networks. Feedback provides reinforcement and thereby supports us as we move through the action component of the strategic process. It also provides a forum in

which we can find creative solutions to problems that may arise and to fears we may be facing.

3. **Be flexible.** During the evaluation process, we must remain open to change. Our action plan will need to be added to, modified and refined in order to remain effective. We will continue to make use of our powers of discernment to direct planning and action in the future.

In the past, many people saw planning strategies as straightjackets. This is a totally ineffective approach: we must be open to change at any point. We act, we assess, we change. Each time we act, we learn something, and we must use what we have learned to guide our future planning and activity.

4. **Celebrate.** We must remember to congratulate ourselves on our accomplishments, and to acknowledge our progress through the action plan. By reminding ourselves that we are indeed making headway toward our goals, we build the confidence that creates ongoing momentum.

A School for One

Over the course of our lives, we cannot help but learn an enormous amount on a variety of subjects. When our day-to-day learning takes place in the context of our own goals and visions, our learning becomes even more valuable.

We are creating our own individual futures, and no one can teach us exactly how they should unfold. We can think of the strategic process as a customized "school for one."

We are both teacher and student. Our purpose is to manage the complexities of the lives we have chosen, and our goals and objectives make up the curriculum. It is up to us to decide on the course of study and the learning activities that will take place, to evaluate the results, and then to make adjustments that will allow future actions to become increasingly effective.

As is true in any school, it is important to focus continually on our progress. When we concentrate only on the distance still to go before our long-term objectives are reached, we can feel discouraged and defeated. If, however, we constantly note how far forward we have moved, our record of accomplishment provides us with the impetus to continue to make progress.

It is essential to *remain strategic* as we accomplish short-term goals. We must continually evaluate our progress, and make use of our discernment to tell us where we have been successful in remaining on course, and where revisions and adjustments will be needed in the future.

The Crossroads

After weeks and months of developing our great vision, it is humbling to have to go back to the beginning and start to plan the small steps that will help us to reach what we have envisioned for ourselves. However, the difference between success and failure is whether or not we are willing to take responsibility for the part of the process which brings our dreams to life.

We cannot sit back and wait for others to make this happen for us. We have not earned our dreams simply by envisioning them. The world owes us nothing. The Promise is no more.

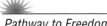

At the moment we cross the line from planning to implementation, we have begun the process that will transform us. That first planned action is a statement. With that first step — and each one that follows — we are announcing our own responsibility for the future. We are accepting that we are the authority on how our own life will evolve, and how it will be evaluated. By acknowledging that there is no one else to depend on or to blame, we are leaving behind the entitlement perspective. We are saying, "This is my vision. I am willing to do the work to accomplish it."

It is during the strategic process — discernment, planning, action, evaluation, discernment, planning, action, evaluation — that the Inner and the External Entrepreneurs in each of us meet. This is a critical moment, as it allows us to move from the spiritual to the material aspects of our lives, making use of both of them at once. This integration of essence and pragmatism creates the holistic approach to life which is essential to success. It puts us on the road to freedom.

CHAPTER FOUR

The Risk Factor

Through understanding our relationship with risk, we become aware of how this important factor can help or hinder us as we move forward into strong entrepreneurial positions.

> **"The paradox of courage is that a man must be a little careless of his life even in order to keep it."**
> — *G.K. Chesterton*

Our comfort levels with risk are very much determined by our individual attitudes and experiences, and these vary tremendously from one person to the next. Some people seem to welcome risk in all sectors of their lives, while others are uncomfortable with any kind of change. Most of us are somewhere in between. In addition, all of us approach risk differently at different times in our lives, and under different circumstances.

It is natural to feel apprehensive when we contemplate major life changes that will alter our prospects for the future. There is a space between where we are and where we want to be, and at times it can seem enormous. Our fear of that space — which represents the unknown — is essentially our fear of risk.

We can find plenty of possible scenarios in that gap to worry about. If our attitudes become more entrepreneurial but we remain in our current positions, how will we relate to our employers and our fellow workers? If we leave comfortable employment to start a business, what will happen to our incomes? What effect will a dramatic change in us have on our families?

What if, in trying to transform ourselves, we lose our security? Our identity?

These last questions are, of course, the big ones. The fear we feel when we contemplate change and the unknown is essentially a fear of loss. Risk makes us vulnerable to loss, and while we are able to imagine the possibilities for gain and growth that risk and change can offer us, we can also imagine what we might lose.

Managing the Fear of Risk

It is important to remember what powerful visualizers humans are. We can use our vision to create futures for ourselves that are filled with self-confidence and success, or we can use it to imagine all of the things that could possibly go wrong along the path to freedom. Which course we take is closely connected to the level of our self-confidence.

When we lack confidence, our imaginations can make the future seem riskier than it is, and can blow the possibilities for loss far out of real proportion. Imagining a future in which we fail to surmount obstacles is guaranteed to erode our confidence. The more negative circumstances we imagine for the future, the greater our fear, and the more diminished our ability to move forward.

When our confidence is solid, on the other hand, we can envision the positive steps we must take to overcome the obstacles and challenges that may confront us. Our confidence gives us the faith to move forward, and each obstacle we face and surmount increases our confidence even further.

As we work with our Inner Entrepreneurs to transform our attitudes and our behavior to better meet the future, we will enter the "risk zone" frequently. Each time we do so, we must be aware of the dichotomy: we can have faith that we will be able to create successful circumstances for ourselves, and receive power from this faith, or we can fear how we may react to negative circumstances, and let the fear erode our power. The choice is always ours.

Levels of Risk-Taking

Confidence is a worthy opponent to the fear of risk. The greater the risk — as we perceive it — the greater the self-confidence that is required. Common sense tells us that there is no point in taking risks that we know our self-confidence cannot yet manage — or risks that we have no interest in managing. The choices we make and the speed with which we implement change in our lives must relate to our own personal levels of comfort. Each person's decision is the right decision for them.

Risk Level One

It is possible to be an entrepreneur on the inside while making relatively few external changes. Level One risk-takers — we can think of them as "Intrapreneurs" — find it necessary to make only small adjustments to their existing circumstances in order to work toward personal freedom. A waiter may start thinking of marketing strategies that will help her employer, for example, or a hospital photographer may begin to approach his work as if it were a small business venture within the institutional framework.

These people know they are most comfortable working within the context of an organization whose overall direction has been determined by other people. In favourable circumstances, their employers will also be moving toward an overall organizing structure that allows greater self-direction for employees.

As individuals at Level One develop entrepreneurial attitudes, they will find themselves rethinking their jobs. They will enjoy greater accountability and assume increasing responsibility for their own work within the organizational context. They will bring creativity and energy to their work, making them more valuable to themselves and others. They will, in short, exercise their own entrepreneurial spirit within existing organizations to create vocations out of jobs.

The risk at Level One is primarily internal, and carried out in small initiatives.

Risk Level Two

Level Two is an interim level of risk. Again this level may meet the need for independence for some individuals for all time. Others will see it as a mid-point on the way to complete self-direction. At this level, the entrepreneur will find certain security in employment or within organizing structures developed by others, while at the same time beginning to enjoy some of the benefits of independence.

Examples of Level Two risk-takers are people who rely in part on commissions for their incomes. Level Two individuals may also work at one job to earn an income while building a totally different vocation during early mornings, evenings and weekends, with the goal of ultimate self-employment in their area of vocational interest. Craftspeople and artists have often done this, but it is a viable option for people with a variety of other vocational interests as well.

Other examples of Level Two risk include network marketing and franchises. These kinds of enterprise allow the individual to develop independence while operating under a pre-determined organizing structure.

Although Level Two risk is greater than that of Level One, which means that there are more areas where control must be relinquished, some security and permanence is still built into the organizing structure — at least for the time being.

Risk Level Three

Risk Level Three is total economic independence. Individuals at this stage have created their own organizing structures, and have made the move to self-employment in order to implement them. Level Three individuals operate from their own, self-determined set of rules, and they do not rely on the organizing structures of others.

Level Three risk takers are external, as well as internal, entrepreneurs. As they move toward total independence for their own futures, their risk level is the highest. So is their possibility for freedom and reward.

Emergency Care for the No-Choice Move

Occasionally individuals will move from one risk level to another because of changes in the organizing structures of their places of employment. People who were working at Level Two may suddenly realize they have been moved to Level One. This may happen due to growth and change — or downsizing and takeovers — within the business or industry itself.

Alternately, those who have been contentedly working at Level One may find themselves at Level Two — due, again, to forces outside themselves. More and more businesses are encouraging independence within their organizational structures. This may be due to a genuine desire to move toward more creative working environments, where individuals are given opportunities for independence and imagination. But it may also be due to economics: a disinclination by employers to pay health benefits and pensions can result in more contract and commissioned positions, and fewer full-time employment positions. This is a good thing as far as some employees are concerned, but an unwelcome change for others.

The most difficult scenarios — and they are all too common in these economic times — are the ones in which individuals find themselves with no apparent options at all. Their positions may have been terminated, and it may be necessary for them to use their severance packages and savings to somehow establish themselves again.

The shock of losing a job can be devastating to one's confidence. However, as we disengage from The Promise and become free of entitlement thinking, losing a job can also be liberating. The period which follows the loss can be profoundly meaningful if we use it to reevaluate our vocational progress and choose to align our futures more closely with our life missions.

The key to survival in such circumstances is to respond — and not to react — to the current situation. Scheduling a Strategic Time Out is a genuinely constructive way to respond to losing a job — or to being shifted from one position to another — against our will. We must allow ourselves to disengage from the confusion of the present circumstances, to put those circumstances into context, and to draw on the wisdom of the Inner Entrepreneur.

The following "911" procedure can assist in strategizing the way out of a no-choice move:

1. Seek the advice of others you trust. These may be people who have successfully moved through similar situations, and people who believe in you and your unique talents.

2. Avoid past-focused ("Why me?"), entitlement and negative conversations with others, and with yourself. Direct your thoughts and actions toward the future, rather than the past.

3. Ask yourself, "If I were counselling someone who was experiencing what I have just experienced, what would be my first item of advice?"

4. Ask yourself, "What key areas do I need to focus on in order to find a pathway through these present circumstances?" Key areas that require your attention may include family members and

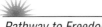
others in your personal support system, your finances and your health, as well as potential new sources of income.

5. Spend time assessing each of the key focus areas you have identified, and ask yourself, "What needs to happen in each area during the next two weeks to move me closer to my overall goals?"

6. Develop an action plan for the next three months, made up of smaller, two-week steps, that will help you to reach your goals in each of the key areas you have identified.

7. Share the plan with people you trust... and ask for their support in accomplishing the outcomes of your plan.

Implementing Change

It is important for each individual who is contemplating the steps that lead to change to remember that it is not necessary to implement all change at once. The opportunity exists for each of us to move gradually, taking one small risk-taking step after another. As we do this, our confidence in our ability to succeed at change increases, which gives us greater power for implementing change in the future. Although we cannot avoid risk completely, no matter how well prepared we are — nor do we want to do so — we need to be sensible in order to protect ourselves from unnecessary loss. It is valuable to consider alternatives and to explore possibilities when contemplating difficult choices, in order to minimize our risk.

It is also true that those who take risks do not always succeed. It is worthwhile to remember that those who succeed at everything they try are rarely taking any risks at all. An old saw says, "Nothing ventured, nothing gained." Unfortunately, many of us have learned that "to not succeed" means the same thing as "to fail."

"Failure" is a matter of interpretation. If we look at life with confidence, there is really no such thing as failure; there are only opportunities to grow and learn. Nothing is ever lost — and learning from those things that did not work as well as we had hoped is part of the life-long process of education.

By moving forward into the unfamiliar territory that will help us to reach our goals, we free ourselves from the perception of fear by replacing it with experience. Through experience, we turn fear into fuel.

The Leap of Faith

Each of us must understand and respect our own unique relationship with risk. Through listening to our inner voices, we can become aware of the aspects of risk which can be fully strategized and planned, and those where some courage will be required.

We need courage when there are no clear or controllable outcomes, and the road to full self-direction will occasionally require courage from each of us. When we encounter such circumstances, our best option is to live in the moment — to get through the transition and out the other side. This requires a leap of faith. We know ourselves, we know the decision we have made is right for us. We must have faith in our own abilities, and in the positive nature of the outcome.

When we overcome fears and rise to meet challenges, we enrich the growing medium from which our energy comes. These small acts build our confidence and our experience, and lead to greater confidence, creativity and growth. Creativity leads to risk. Risk leads to learning, and to success. Success gives us confidence and stimulates our creativity for future enterprise. We cannot acquire this kind of energy in any other way.

PUTTING YOUR FREEDOM TO WORK FOR YOU

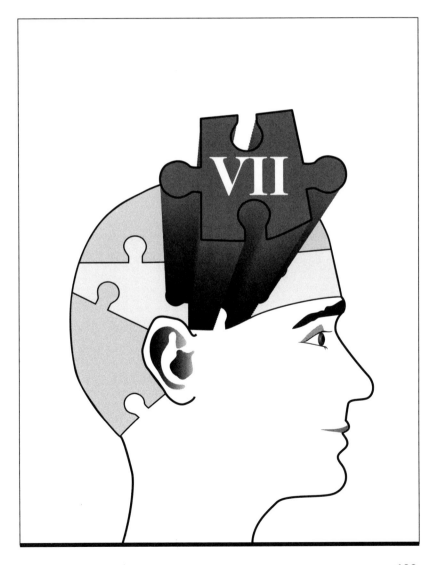

VII

Putting Your Freedom to Work for You

> "There are risks and costs to a program of action. But they are far less than the long-range risks of comfortable inaction."
>
> *— John F. Kennedy*

We have a growing awareness of who we are as individuals. We are beginning to see what we can become. We know that history has presented us with an unequalled opportunity for personal growth and transformation.

We know that we will be taking risks by moving forward, but we know we would prefer to take those risks than be bogged down in the past. We have learned how to manage fear, and put it to work for us.

There comes a point when we are as prepared as we can be, a point where we must move forward. At that point, the work of the Inner Entrepreneur starts to become external, and we begin to move through physical time toward the unfolding of our visions.

CHAPTER ONE

The Entrepreneurial Setting

⊱─┤◆⟩─○─⟨◆├─┤⊰

While there are likely as many variations on the entre-preneurial setting as there are entrepreneurial individuals, four basic patterns can be identified: the independent entrepreneurship, entrepreneurship within a pre-established structure, entrepreneurship within an existing organization, and entrepreneurship within the not-for-profit setting.

⟶⥤◉⥢⟵

Go confidently in the direction of your dreams.
Live the life you have imagined.

— *Henry David Thoreau*

⟶⥤◉⥢⟵

Independent Entrepreneurship

Fully independent entrepreneurs — those working with the greatest level of risk — have almost unlimited freedom to seek economic independence through the use of their creativity and talents in the creation of value for others. These people also have flexibility when it comes to exploring and creating the personal organizing structures that best support their personal growth and priorities.

Independent entrepreneurs have developed enough self-confidence to overcome — or put to use — the fears that are associated with relinquishing traditional avenues of security. They are able to apply their time and energy to activities that will bring them closer to their own definitions of personal fulfillment and life significance.

Entrepreneurship within a Pre-Established Structure

The opportunities for entrepreneurism offered within pre-established structures are appealing options for some. Network marketing and franchise ownership are two examples of this type of structure.

Network marketing can serve as a pathway for many individuals in becoming more entrepreneurial without having the responsibility for developing all the details of a complex organizing structure. Since network marketing can be carried out on a part-time basis, it can be a viable, yet flexible option. In some cases, network marketing ventures are so successful that they become full-time businesses.

Franchise operations can offer a range of options for entrepreneurial independence. Some are very highly structured and controlled, while others allow their owners greater flexibility.

Entrepreneurship within an Organization

For-profit organizations can be conducive environments for individual employees who are willing to accept moderate levels of risk in exchange for the opportunity to develop their entrepreneurial skills.

"Intrapreneurship" is most successful when the established organization is willing to create a working context that allows individual creativity to flourish, and promotes the development of relationships, skills and initiatives. This structure depends on teamwork, and it results in increased value to the organization and its customers.

Organizations that facilitate the development of intrapreneurial skills tend to focus on results more than on time and energy. The intrapreneur assumes increased financial risk when straight salary structures are replaced by result-based performance incentives.

Although organizational rules may limit the options of intrapreneurs to develop and put into practice their own organizing structures, this is often still a viable option to being self-employed. In the current economic climate, as businesses seek creative ways to keep costs down, increasing numbers of opportunities present themselves to those who wish a measure of independence within established organizations.

Entrepreneurship in the Not-for-Profit Setting

The not-for-profit environment can also provide opportunities for the spirit of enterprise to flourish. "To create value for others" is not only the basic principle of entrepreneurship, it is also the watchword of the not-for-profit organization.

Not-for-profit organizations often provide working environments in which people can actualize their potential. While the contributions are generally volunteer or low paying, significant creativity and progress can be made as the individual applies the talents of his or her Inner Entrepreneur in the not-for-profit setting. In this case, outcomes are measured not financially but in terms of greater service to the community and self-fulfillment.

Employees of not-for-profit organizations have similar opportunities as those working in the corporate community to develop their entrepreneurial skills, despite the normally lower economic return. The visions of the most successful employees in such settings coincide with the visions of the organizations themselves. In working for the betterment of communities or nations, such individuals embody the true spirit of entrepreneurial initiative in their efforts to improve the lives of others.

Those who work as volunteers in not-for-profit organizations also represent the spirit of enterprise, in their donation of time, energy, and resources. Through such donations, they declare themselves on a very personal level, and then actualize their declarations through their actions.

A Special Note on Family Businesses

The family business can serve as a tremendous opportunity for founders, successors and other family members to bring their dreams to life in the spirit of enterprise. However, it is also a setting that can be confusing and very complex from an entrepreneurial perspective.

Much has been written on specific elements of the family business, ranging from developing a succession plan to resolving family conflict. There are several additional aspects to the family-business environment that can affect the development of the individual entrepreneur.

1. Successors in family businesses often work within the context of the founder's organizing structure and vision while still assuming responsibility for becoming an entrepreneur. Three different routes to the future cross and converge in a family business: the pathway of the individual family member, the pathway of family collectively, and the pathway of the business itself. Unfortunately, the best route for the individual may not be the best one for the family, or for the business. In the confusion, successors — and sometimes their spouses — can become "job fillers" rather than "vocation builders," and never be free to establish visions of their own.

2. Because of the complexity of the family-business environment, and the range of expectations that successors and founders may have, a lot of time and energy tends to be wasted on self-justification. This often results in unnecessary competition

among family members. Furthermore, when significant time is spent justifying positions, compensation, and progress, there is little time or energy left to develop individual or collective visions.

3. Every person moving toward self-actualization needs to be alone, away from family members for a period of time, in order to "quest" and to move forward. While short-term retreats may partially fulfill this need, successors in a family business may also need extended periods during which they experience a whole new personal or business environment. Individual quests can be perturbing to any family, as they often signal fundamental changes within the questing individual, and the possibility of changes in family relations. Although individual initiative can be particularly unsettling in the family business environment, successors are more likely to make a significant contribution to the long-term viability of the business if their visions are aligned with, but not a consequence of, the vision of the family business and its founder.

Most members of family businesses recognize that it is necessary on a regular basis to redefine and sharpen the vision of the company as a whole. Supporting successors as they take the time they need to find their individual visions and life missions is an important part of this process. When circumstances are created that allow this to happen, it is a tribute to the family's ability to respect that there are different definitions of — and different pathways to — freedom.

CHAPTER TWO

Keeping Your Vision in Focus

⊱⊶◦⊷⊰

While it is far too early to predict the ultimate consequences of this Fourth Great Crossover, the trends identified in this book can give us the direction we may need to make the best possible use of our current opportunities.

Individuals and organizational managers who view the future, and their contributions to creating and shaping it, with the following points in mind, will maximize their likelihood for a harmonious long-term role in the new world order.

1. We must fall in love with the questions.

In a time when answers change as quickly as the capabilities of the microchip expand, we can no longer afford to deal with the world on the basis of absolutes. We must begin to focus more and more on process — and on asking the right questions on an ongoing basis — rather on finding answers that will endure for all time.

When we fall in love with the questions, we build our confidence in the learning process, rather than on the results of learning. Through this approach, we gain tolerance and maturity, and prepare ourselves to face the additional periods of transition that the future will certainly bring.

As we become more responsible for our own thinking, we become aware that our options need not be limited by our past thinking. We must remain open and flexible in the future as well, in order to be able to take advantage of the opportunities life may offer us.

2. We must develop a positive relationship with our work.

Work is healthy and, despite our complaints and concerns, most of us would choose employment over idleness, and earned incomes over handouts. Each of us has our own relationship with work, and how we relate to the work we do is a personal decision. Today, we can choose to boost our self-esteem and shape our future freedom by contributing value through our work.

The average individual will spend 90,000 hours of his or her lifetime at work. It is up to each of us to ensure that those hours are significant, and that they confirm and support the direction and the progress of our individual life missions.

3. We must become individually responsible for creating value.

All of us, as responsible human beings, occasionally wonder how effectively we have used our time and effort in the past. We all wish to live lives of significance, and we measure that significance in part by examining the relationship between our inner spirit and our actions, and in part by considering the effects of our actions on others.

In order to determine whether we are making a difference in the world, we examine how well we have used
our ability to create value for ourselves and others —
how well, in other words, we have put the Entrepreneurial Principle to work.

The value we create for others with small acts of kindness
in our day-to-day lives are as important as winning gold

> ## "Don't be a man of success, be a man of value."
> — *Albert Einstein*

medals, inventing life-saving drugs, or making financial
contributions to charities. The important component of
creating value is the method we use to do it, and how
well aligned that method is with our own unique blend
of talents, abilities and inclinations.

The range of instruments available to individuals who
wish to create lives of significance and value has never
been greater. Each of us can take responsibility for making a difference to the world, and then choose how we
wish to make our contribution.

**4. We must use our creativity and the significant relation-
ships in our lives to remain engaged in the world.**

Continual technological advances can confuse and
undermine our efforts to come to terms with our own
individual human natures. This is an unsettling period.
It requires us essentially to invent our own world, and to
determine how we will interact with it.

While it is tempting to retreat from a rapidly changing world, it is only by making use of our creativity and developing the spirit of enterprise that we will be able to remain contributing members of the current global transformation. We can make use of our creativity to reinforce our vision for the world, while at the same time remaining open to the wealth of options that present themselves as the new world order takes form.

It is reassuring to remember that the world is made up of individual relationships, and that the more significant these are, the better. While some people seem to have adapted to the age of the microchip by developing more open relationships with their computers and bank machines than they have with friends and family members, our ability to connect with others remains an essential way to create a meaningful and significant life for ourselves and for those around us.

"Cocooning" in terms of scheduling strategic retreats alone and with our life partners is an important part of our development as entrepreneurs. But we must resist the urge to cocoon as a reaction to confusion or discouragement. We can change the status quo only by connecting with others. Such connections will bring not only economic advancement but, more importantly, meaning and grace to our lives.

6. We must personalize the Entrepreneurial Principle.

When religious organizing structures predominated, one did not have to be a priest or a rabbi to make a meaningful contribution to society. It was not only politicians and bureaucrats who flourished during periods of political domination. Similarly, we do not all need to be sole proprietors to be effective economic citizens and sovereign individuals in the new economic organizing structure.

The essential element of holistic fulfilment for the future is the assumption of economic responsibility by each individual, and the application of the entrepreneurial spirit in the creation of value. This may be successfully accomplished at whatever level of initiative is right for each individual.

7. We must accept that we were born to choose.

Before we can establish the organizing structures that will lead to individual freedom and success, we must be utterly convinced of our ability to choose our own future.

In the words of the late Leland Val Van De Wall, noted speaker and writer in the motivational field, we were born to choose what we want and how we will obtain it. We were endowed with the intelligence, the talent and the spirit to be able to achieve our goals. By combining these gifts with the conviction that our visions *can* become realities, we acknowledge our responsibility to make our own choices.

8. We must have faith in synergy and magic.

The choice to become truly entrepreneurial is not an easy one, and the choice is only the beginning. As we move toward self-fulfilment, independence and freedom, there will be times when we are thwarted and frustrated. We may find gulleys of mud and fallen trees and numerous other roadblocks in our way. At times, we will be convinced that we have taken the wrong direction, and that we will never manage to reach our goals.

Times like these are times for faith in synergy and magic. Some of us will invoke them through prayer, and some through visualization. Some of us will turn our backs, not daring to hope — nor even to imagine — that anything good can happen.

But it will.

Over and over again, those who have worked toward bringing their visions to life have recounted tales of being saved by unanticipated cheques, new clients, unexpected opportunities. Call it synergy — call it magic — it happens. And while we can't sit back and wait for it, when we have worked ourselves to the limits of our capacity and found ourselves yet again on the edge of the abyss, just in time the synergy and magic will arrive that will set us on firm footing once again.

What Legacy Will We Leave?

> "Tribal teachings say that you are responsible for future generations because you are the ancestors of the future. Whatever you do today will affect the next seven generations."
>
> — *Jamie Sams*

Imagine that you suddenly find yourself — with your 20th century mind still inside your head — on a pier in southern England. The year is 1495. The printing press has only been in existence for about fifty years. As the Third Great Crossover begins, the majority of people still believe that the world is flat.

Because you come from their future, you feel compelled to give the group of people who are with you on that pier some sense of how the world will be changed by the Third Great Crossover period. But how do you do it? How do you begin to explain all of the technological advancements, the medical breakthroughs, the economic restructuring, the periods of religious and cultural intolerance and tolerance, the inventions and achievements in navigation and communication?

How do you capture the changes in thinking that will occur when the average person realizes that the world they are so familiar with is not flat, but spherical — and that there are other worlds to visit? How do you communicate the democratic processes that will contribute to the emancipation of so many humans? How do you describe the art, the literature, and the music that will be created to reflect the evolution of a world these people barely know about?

How do you explain that a nation that has yet to be "invented" by western civilization — in a land far out of sight on the horizon, beyond that place where the world drops off to nothing — will assume a central role in the new world order, and will serve as a catalyst to change the face of politics around the globe?

Obviously, you cannot.

Today we are as challenged to foresee the future as were our fifteenth-century predecessors. Our pier may be only "virtually" real, but from it we look out over a global horizon and consider the possibilities. What would our descendents be able to communicate to us about the progress, the innovations, and the freedom that will emerge as the effects of the Fourth Great Crossover sweep through every aspect of life and civilization? We cannot know the answers.

However, we do know that ultimately the message we would relate to best is likely the same one our ancestors would have appreciated most if we had been able to pass it back to them. They would have been less concerned about the specific changes the future would bring to technology, the sciences, the arts and other components of daily existence than they would have been to know that their lives were not mere transactions in the course of human evolution. They would have wanted the reassurance that, as individuals and as members of a civilization, they had played a crucial role in a positive transformation of the world.

Like us, our ancestors would have wanted to hear that the difficult work they had faced, both individually and as communities, was recognized centuries later for its pioneering spirit, and that the courage and faith they undertook in all fields of human endeavor was valued by those who came after them.

By declaring ourselves to be actors rather than observers of the changes in the world today, we tap into the power of the Fourth Great Crossover, and allow it to permeate every aspect of our lives. The same kind of synergy inspired and enhanced the work of those who chose to act during the Third Great Crossover period, and led them to the significant advances from which we, at the edge of the Fourth, have benefited.

In the end, the story of the future all humans want to hear is the one that only we as individuals can write — one in which we advance the spirit of greater human freedom, significance, and quality of life through the expression of our creativity, and the employment of our unique abilities and skills.

The entrepreneurial spirit is being awakened in a variety of new forms today — all of them fed by compelling visions. Whether in business, science, the arts or any other field, the goals of entrepreneurial initiative are the same — greater personal responsibility, greater self-knowledge, greater connection to one's work, the inspiration and sustenance that comes from significant relationships, and the creation of a meaningful legacy on which future generations can build.

About the Authors

Patrick Duffy and Adrienne Arlen Duffy are popular consultants, speakers and workshop facilitators. Their company, *Big Futures Inc.*, provides organizational and communications expertise to a broad client base throughout North America. *Big Futures* assists individuals, groups and organizations to develop entrepreneurial initiative, focus on strategic processes, and learn to manage change. The company also designs and implements comprehensive training programs on behalf of clients.

Patrick was born and raised in Canada; Adrienne is a native of the United States. Both were independent entrepreneurs before establishing their creative partnership in 1984. The Duffys and their young daughter live in Canada.

For more information on:

▶ **Pathway to Freedom Workbook**

▶ **Pathway to Freedom Workshops**

▶ **The Corporate Services of Big Futures Inc.**

Phone: **(403) 487-7571**
Fax: **(403) 489-7562**

Address: **Big Futures Inc.**
          P.O. Box 78115
          6655 - 178 Street
          Edmonton, Alberta
          T5T 6A1

Pathway to Freedom

O R D E R   F O R M

Name _____

Company _____

Address _____

_____

City _____ Province or State _____

Postal Code or Zip Code _____

Phone (   ) _____ Fax (   ) _____

QUANTITY	ITEM DESCRIPTION	PRICE EACH	TOTAL
	Pathway to Freedom		
Regular Price . . . .$21.95 each**		**Sub-total**	
Discounts available for multiple copies:		S & H	
6-10 copies @ 10% discount = $19.75 each** 11-20 copies @ 20% discount = $17.50 each**		7% GST*	
20+ copies @ 30% discount = $15.40 each**		**TOTAL**	

*   *Add 7% GST if you are ordering from a Canadian address.*
** *Please call for the cost of shipping and handling to your location.*

Please charge my:

☐ VISA   ☐ Master Card

Your credit card will NOT be charged until books are shipped.

Card No. _____

Expiry Date _____

Signature _____

☐ **YES**, I want more information on *Pathway to Freedom* knowledge
products, seminars, and workshops.

To order, fax this form to **(403) 489-7562**

or contact us directly at   **Big Futures Inc.**
                                     P.O. Box 78115
                                       6655 - 178 Street
                                       Edmonton, AB T5T 6A1
                                       Phone (403) 487-7571

Pathway to Freedom

O R D E R   F O R M

Name _____

Company _____

Address _____

_____

City _____ Province or State _____

Postal Code or Zip Code _____

Phone (   ) _____ Fax (   ) _____

QUANTITY	ITEM DESCRIPTION	PRICE EACH	TOTAL
	Pathway to Freedom		

Regular Price . . . .$21.95 each**	**Sub-total**	
Discounts available for multiple copies:	S & H	
6-10 copies @ 10% discount = $19.75 each** 11-20 copies @ 20% discount = $17.50 each**	7% GST*	
20+ copies @ 30% discount = $15.40 each**	**TOTAL**	

*   *Add 7% GST if you are ordering from a Canadian address.*
** *Please call for the cost of shipping and handling to your location.*

Please charge my:

☐ VISA   ☐ Master Card

Your credit card will NOT be charged until books are shipped.

Card No. _____

Expiry Date _____

Signature _____

☐ **YES**, I want more information on *Pathway to Freedom* knowledge products, seminars, and workshops.

To order, fax this form to **(403) 489-7562**

or contact us directly at   **Big Futures Inc.**
P.O. Box 78115
6655 - 178 Street
Edmonton, AB T5T 6A1
Phone (403) 487-7571